Amish Voices

of Harmony

Collected and written by
Drucilla Milne, Harmony, Minnesota

Disclaimer: Members of the Amish community have a religious proscription against having their pictures taken. The Ten Commandments provide a guideline for them in leading Christian lives, and the second Commandment in Deut.5:8 states: "You shall not make for yourself a graven image, or any likeness of anything that is in heaven above, or that is on the earth beneath, or that is in the water under the earth." In upholding this Commandment, not only do the Amish object to having their pictures taken, they do not own or use cameras or any other mechanisms for capturing images. It is also the reason there are no faces on Amish dolls or mirrors in Amish homes, except for a small mirror which men use for shaving.

Out of respect for this belief, the pictures I have used for the book dividers are of English children posing as Amish children.

Illustrator

Eileen Gierke, who is now retired, lives in the Harmony area with her husband Dave on a thirteen acre hobby farm. Eileen is able to spend more time pursuing her artistic talents. Although her children and her grandchildren are some of her favorite subjects, she has been commissioned to do several portraits where individual photographs have been combined to produce a family portrait. She has also done portraits taking favorite pets and their masters and with individual pictures has been able to create a lasting memory. Eileen's interest in my book and her artistic abilities led me to ask for her help with the illustrations.

Since Amish belief prohibited us from taking pictures of the Amish children, we chose to use our grandchildren as models—two of Eileen's grandchildren, Nicole and Rebecca Bryce and two of my great-grandchildren, Michael and Ariannah Barrett. The illustrations were based on photography taken in the Harmony area. I can't thank Eileen enough for her support, friendship, and artistic contribution.

Copyright 2007   Printed by Davies Printing Co., Rochester, MN. 2007   Third printing

Amish Voices of Harmony

Preface

Reasons for Amish Settlement in Southeastern Minnesota

During the early 1970s in Wayne County, Ohio, the Amish were being crowded out both commercially and by overpopulation. It was time to look for new land, to begin a new community of Amish. Delegations from Ohio made three trips into Wisconsin and/or Minnesota. When they came to the area of Canton and Harmony townships, they liked what they saw—wooded areas with timber for building and for fuel, natural springs as a water source for animals and for cooling milk, small acreage farms, rich soil with good drainage. At this time, land prices were also reasonable, one acre selling for approximately $300 to $700.

Another factor of great importance to the Amish was the state laws regarding education. They found that Minnesota permitted the schooling of children through Grade 8 in one-room schoolhouses. The state also allowed the Amish an exemption from the law mandating school attendance until the age of sixteen.*

Satisfied with the land, the environs, and the accommodation of state laws, the Amish bought their first farm in the area in December of 1973 and the family moved onto the farm in March of 1974.

The Amish population in Southeastern Minnesota continuously experiences change. Many of the families who were newcomers to this area have moved on to join other Amish communities. When young Amish couples marry, they sometimes choose to join other communities; the parents and grandparents may then move as well to remain close to their families. Other reasons for resettlement include overcrowding, the influx of tourism, and a lack of land.

The underlying mobility of the Amish seems to create an endless flow, a constant moving and looking for new land and areas to settle.

---

* Minnesota Dept. of Education, 1991 Education Laws, Volume 1, Chapters 117-125   Extract from 1991 Minnesota Statutes, printed January 1992

Part I

Getting to Know Our Amish Neighbors

Introduction

GETTING TO KNOW OUR AMISH NEIGHBORS

Introduction

My husband Loren and I lived on a farm north of Harmony for almost forty years before we built a home in Harmony. The Amish became our neighbors during the1970s when they began moving into this area from Ohio in 1974. Our friendship with the Amish grew out of the simplicity of my visits to purchase eggs and garden produce that I didn't grow in my own garden.

Visiting their homes was like entering a different time zone. I felt a certain comfort and peacefulness especially in the evening when darkness was approaching. The soft glow and smell of the kerosene lamps added to the quiet, restful atmosphere. The ticking of the clock and the night sounds were undisturbed by the sounds of modern life—the television, the air conditioner, the refrigerator, etc. In the quietness of their homes, I could hear the sound of animals, birds, crickets, the wind and the rustle of branches and leaves in the trees.

From these early friendships and visiting with my Amish friends while I was writing my first book, I gained many insights into the lifestyle of their community. As my understanding of their lifestyle grew and my relationship with them deepened, I earned—very slowly and with careful consideration and respect for their privacy—a small degree of trust. This trust was exemplified when I was first asked twenty years ago to be a guide for the newly created Amish tours. I went to an Amish friend and said, "I've been asked to do tours in your community. I want to know how you feel about it."

"Rather you than someone else," was the reply. This simple remark has stayed with me for years because of the trust and friendship it conveyed.

I have many stories to share that show this community's lifestyle, family values and humor. As I did with my first book, I have gathered information and anecdotes very slowly, carefully, and directly from the Amish. My approach involves interviewing individuals, compiling the information into book format, then returning to read what I have written to the individuals involved. In this way, all of the material included in my books was approved by the Amish before printing. So that the people and their identities will not be apparent, the stories may be changed somewhat and I will not use the full names of the individuals.

It has taken me a long time to decide whether to write another book because the Amish are a closed community and individuals do not like to be singled out. While I greatly respect the significance of this view, I also believe it is important that the general public understand our common human likenesses, even though we live totally different lifestyles. Both English (as the Amish call anyone outside their community) and Amish try to lead lives pleasing to God and we share many Bible-based beliefs. Our lifestyles may differ but our love for family, humor about life and interdependence are the same.

A core belief of the Amish that sets them apart from us is that they live "in the world" but do not want to be "of the world." This concept is based on the Bible and can be found in such verses as: 1 John 2:15-18—"Do not love the world or the things in the world...the world passes away...but he who does the will of God abides forever."

The Amish believe that such Bible passages call them to a life of separation and self-denial. Rom.12: Verse 1, as paraphrased in *The One Bible Commentary* says, "God's redeeming love should be answered by the true and spiritual ritual service of a life of purity and self-denial and work for God." Verse 2 adds, "Do not follow the fashions and customs of the worldly society around you, but let your ways of thinking be so changed by the Holy Spirit that you look for and recognize God's will and love to do it."

The Amish thus believe that they can best serve God by eliminating the things of the world and living a life of self-denial without the temptations and entrapments of a modern world. Although some Amish sects are more liberal than others, the group in the Harmony/Canton area is known as "Old Order" Amish, meaning least progressive. Their homes have no electricity, and they have no automobiles or tractors.

To contemporary society the Amish may seem to be going backwards instead of forward because the choices they make always limit progress. The changes that do come into 'their world' are brought in quietly and very slowly. Even then, changes are viewed with much trepidation, especially by the older generations. Referring to progress, Old Bishop Jake, the oldest bishop in our local group, once said to me, "It's like falling off a roof. You can't stop the fall anymore than you can stop progress."

Part II

Times Have Brought Change

Vernon Michel and Amish Tourism

Tourism Reaches an All-Time High

Tourism and the Old Barn Resort

Tourism and change (1985-2007)

Changes Brought By Time:
The Beginnings of Tourism

When the Ohio Amish moved into the townships of Harmony and Canton in 1974, residents of these small Southeastern townships knew little of the Amish lifestyle. The Amish, however, had lived next door to many English speaking farmers in Ohio and were accustomed to the "English."(This is the term the Amish use for anyone who is not Amish and speaks English. The Amish speak Pennsylvania Dutch.) It soon became a familiar sight to see horse drawn buggies clip clopping down the street, driven by Amish people wearing dark colored clothing. Fields that had once been cultivated with tractors were now being cultivated with horse-drawn machinery. Intrigued by the sights and sounds of this lifestyle from the past, tourists soon started coming to the area. The idea of Amish tourism, however, came about in a rather unexpected way.

Vernon Michel and Amish Tourism

In 1987, promoting tourism in Southeastern Minnesota—also known as "Bluff Country"—required more lodging for tourists in Harmony and the surrounding areas. Vernon Michel, a local farmer, came up with the unique idea of Farm Vacations, where city people could enjoy the adventure of staying on a farm amid the animals, fields, and open skies. He found farm sites within a sixty mile radius of Harmony that would be willing to open their homes and lifestyles to tourists. He also placed an ad in the *Smithsonian* for  Farm Vacations located in the same area in which the Amish had settled. The phone calls began coming in with questions about the Amish.

In an article in the *Minneapolis Star and Tribune* dated August 23, 1987, Catherine Watson wrote, "His (Vernon Michel's) original idea was Michel's Farm Vacations—a group of carefully screened farm homes that would take guests for one night to a week or more in a farm setting."[1] Later on in this same article, Watson captures how almost incidentally the groundwork was laid for Amish tourism: "His

---

1 Catherine Watson, "Amish Country," *Minneapolis Star and Tribune*, August 23, 1987, p. 4E.

original brochure added, rather casually, that the Harmony area has the Upper Midwest's largest Amish Community—about 100 families, roughly the same size as the Amish community in Vernon County, Wisconsin. . . That hit a surprisingly deep nerve of interest." This interest led to the development of Amish tourism in our area.

Capitalizing on the interest shown in Watson's article, Vernon realized that a driving tour in the Amish Countryside with trained guides might be an option. He knew people wanted to experience the Amish lifestyle even if briefly, and this could be done via a driving tour. To make his idea a reality, Vernon went into the Amish community, stopping and talking to several Amish people. He prearranged Amish farms where tourists could stop to purchase baked goods, crafts and see Amish homes and workplaces on these guided driving tours. The first four tour guides were Joan Michel, Marilyn Trouten, Muriel Johnson, and myself, Drucilla Milne.

During our first training session Vernon stopped at Lydia Ann Hershberger's. Lydia Ann was an Amish woman who had been selling baked goods at the side of Highway 52 from her horse-drawn black buggy. Joan Michel was timing the tour to see how long it took to get to Lydia Ann's home. Joan recalled, "We were there at 10:00 AM and Lydia Ann's wall clock said 9:30. Lydia Ann called it 'One-half Time' because the Amish stay on Standard Time when we switch to Daylight Savings Time." Vernon got directly to the point of his visit and asked Lydia Ann if she would be interested in allowing tour groups to stop at her home. She paused only a moment before replying, "You can come in this door and go out that door."

The guides were (and still are) trained to respect the privacy of the Amish and their beliefs. One of these beliefs concerns graven images. In the Bible, Deut.5: 8 states: "You shall not make for yourself a graven image or any likeness of anything that is in heaven above, or that is on the earth beneath, or that is in the water under the earth." The Old Order Amish take this statement literally. Out of consideration for this belief, NO PICTURES or cameras or other devices for capturing their likeness are allowed. The Amish would rather no pictures of any kind—not just of them—be taken, simply because some tourists become too aggressive and overstep the boundaries showing respect for their beliefs.

In October of 1987, Harmony had its annual 'Fall Foliage Festival.' Vernon had suggested to the Harmony Chamber of Commerce that guided tours into the Amish countryside should be one of the activities offered. At first, the Chamber of Commerce could not see how the tours could be done. Not enough guides were available to conduct the tours. The Chamber members came up with an alternative approach—a map that was a self-guided tour of the countryside. These maps identified where many of the Amish families had settled. Two-hundred-and-thirty maps were sold at a minimal fee. Vernon's guides did tours from his place of business, as well. This high rate of response indicated that people were definitely interested in the Amish and their lifestyle.

Tourism Reaches an All-Time High

As 1987 continued, the effects of Catherine Watson's article in the *Minneapolis Star and Tribune* continued to build Amish tourism: "Immediately," Vernon recalled, "nine out of ten calls we got were about the Amish."

According to Joan Michel, who worked for Vernon, "The phone rang off the hook shortly after the article came out. It was wild. Two years later, people still were coming into the store with the paper and article in their hand. The article in the *Minneapolis Star Tribune* was a god-send to the business."

Vernon soon had not only his original four guides, but eighteen more as well, and the demand for tours was still rising. The dramatic increase in Amish tourism continued, and by February of 1997, Vernon was quoted in an article in the *Rochester Post Bulletin* as saying, "About 2000 cars and 216 buses carry tourists to the community each year." [2]

In this same article, Harmony Mayor Chris Skaalen states, "Harmony fills up during the summer because of tourism, which has been the springboard to a renewed downtown and a revitalized economy for the area . . . Much of the credit for the town's tourism growth goes to Vernon Michel, who was the tourism pioneer for the area. Michel proved that if you can market an area's natural and cultural qualities, tourists will come." Skaalen also mentions how some people at first reacted to Vernon's idea for Amish tours: "People thought he was crazy." Typically, however, Vernon thought differently. "I guess I never considered it a risk... In my mind, it was a thing that would go." Time has certainly proven how right Vernon was.

---

2 Jon Weiss, "Here People Really Live In Harmony," *Rochester Post-Bulletin*, February 6, 1997, p. 6B
*(Note of interest: "Michel's Amish Tours" has since been sold and is now "Harmony Amish Tours.")

Tourism: Old Barn Resort
(Remodeled in 1988 / opened 1990)

The Amish also figured prominently in another of Vernon's tourism endeavors: the transformation of a barn into The Old Barn Resort. Originally the barn had been built by Edward Allis, owner of the Allis-Chalmers Company, for his son Jerre. The barn is huge—100 feet long, 50 feet wide and 35 feet in height. The farm was meant to be a dairy farm with imported Holstein cows from England. Allis's son, Jerre, however, added two horse racing tracks and changed the whole atmosphere of the farm. According to legend, the barn once boarded Dan Patch, a championship harness racing horse.

Because of the Allis barn's size, location, and interesting history, Vernon began negotiating with the owners, William J. and Lois Rissman, to purchase the property to promote tourism in the area.

Knowing the high degree of skills that the Amish brought to building, Vernon hired three young Amish men to do the remodeling. At the time Vernon hired them, they were twenty and twenty-one years of age.

The young Amish workers came by horse and buggy fourteen miles from their homes near Canton, Minnesota, every Monday and returned home on Saturday night. Since they worked six days a week, Vernon moved a trailer on site for their use. The prohibition against electricity that is part of the Old Order Amish beliefs was set aside temporarily since the young men were working for Vernon. They were allowed to have a refrigerator—quite a change for them, since the

Amish use ice or circulating well water for cooling. They were also permitted to use the modern plumbing of the trailer.

Some of the first things they were required to do were necessary, menial jobs. For example, there were still cattle in the barn when it was purchased, and the manure that remained in the gutters and box

The Allis barn before remodeling.

stalls had to be removed. The young men were placed wherever they were needed and took on whatever the job required. Some jobs they had never done before, such as tuckpointing the limestone in the lower level of the barn. Milking had been done in this area, and the cattle had licked the mortar from between the limestone blocks. The old wood siding had to be nailed on again because the nails had come loose or had to be replaced. New siding also had to be added. Considering the size of the barn, this was a challenging job.

Everything that could be retained as it had been in the barn was left in its original state. Instead of gutting the inside, partitions were put up to create rooms. At the upper level, the beams were left intact; the Amish boys could be seen walking on the large beams at the very peak of the barn, working where the hayfork and track had once hung. The boys were fearless, walking on beams and tackling jobs at heights where most people would be paralyzed with fear.

In fact, when the time came to clean the Old Barn in preparation for opening day, Vernon hired professional cleaners from Rochester.

They arrived with their equipment, but when they attached their hoses to reach the high ceilings and peaks, they found there was no suction. As Vernon put it, "They weren't comfortable up there—more just hanging on than working." In the meantime, seeing the problem, the three Amish boys got the shop vacuum, climbed onto the high beams in the ceiling, set to work with a fifteen foot hose, and got the cleaning done. Vernon's description of them was, "They were like cats. They walked around up there with no fear."

Besides remodeling the barn itself, the Amish workers built the enclosures for the swimming pool, the well-house, toilets for the campgrounds, and the building for the pressure tanks. They also built the structure that houses the wood-burning unit. Many people have been intrigued by Vernon's ingenuity in devising this wood heating system; it is used to heat the barn as well as the swimming pool.

One of the last jobs the young men had was to shingle the roof of the entire barn. Because of its size, the roof of the barn took sixty squares of shingles— an extraordinary number. The three Amish workers first put on plywood and styrofoam, then the shingles. The shingling was completed in six days. Saturday evening, the young Amish men worked in the moonlight to finish up.

When it came time to paint the barn, Vernon got bids of $2000 and $3000. The Amish wanted to put in a bid as well. Their bid was $1000. Since one of these young men was not twenty-one, his share would have gone to his father, so only the two who were twenty-one did the painting. They rented a spray painter from the Amish Bishop. It was run by a gas engine. Using thirty-foot ladders, they set up scaffolding with brackets to make a platform. Their approach was to set up two ladders, and as they came to the end of the second ladder, they would set up a third. In this way, they could continue spraying, walking from one platform to the next. One of the workers kept the sprayer filled and moved the ladders and platform so that the other one could continue to spray.

Painting the peaks of the barn was a real challenge. The young Amish men again showed ingenuity in getting this portion painted. They got a ten foot boom to do the east wall. They attached a rope to a basket and anchored it to the cupola. One of them then climbed into the basket, while the other one swung the basket back and forth until the spraying was completed.

According to Vernon, "They started on a Monday and were all done with one coat of linseed oil and two coats of paint, using parts of three days to complete the job. It took nineteen gallons of linseed oil and one-hundred and twenty-five gallons of paint."

For Vernon's young laborers, however, working on the Old Barn was not "all work and no play". Vernon remembers how they made a V-blade out of boards they found on the property. With this, they bladed off an area on the Root River so they could ice skate. They invited about twenty Amish friends to their skating parties. Vernon recalls that the young Amish people enjoyed at least three of these parties. The boys worked hard, but they did find time to enjoy the woods, the river and the area. They hunted, fished, innertubed down the Root River, and rode horseback.

These young Amish men did all the necessary work in remodeling the Old Barn, although plumbers and electricians did their part when their expertise was required. When the Amish trio finished, the lower level of the barn had been converted into a hostel with a game room, bunk beds, a laundry area, a kitchen, restrooms and showers. The

Working in the basement of the barn.

upper levels were transformed into a restaurant and bar, a campground office, meeting rooms, a convenience store and a gift shop. In all, the remodeling process took almost two years, beginning in May of 1988 and ending in April of 1990.

During the remodeling, Vernon had the foresight to promote his Old Barn Resort by scheduling buses for tourists to witness the ongoing renovations. A 'long tour' took in the Old Barn Resort as well as the

16

Working together in the basement of the barn.

nearby historic town of Lanesboro, Minnesota. These buses were some of the first tourism buses that went into the area of Lanesboro. Once the Old Barn project was completed, guides would first do a tour of the Amish of the Harmony/Canton area, then have lunch at the Old Barn restaurant, and continue on to tour Lanesboro.

The Old Barn Resort has since been sold to Douglas and Shirley Brenna, originally from Eagan, Minnesota. Besides the campground and the swimming pool, the Resort area offers magnificent scenery, sightseeing, bike trails, the Root River for tubing and fishing, and a recently expanded 18-hole golf course.*

Tourism and Change
(1985 to 2007)

Tourism has brought much needed revenue into the Amish community; however, as I said previously in my book, *The Amish of Harmony,* "the Amish view tourism as a two-edged knife." ** They have become dependent on tourism because land is no longer available to them in small acres, since large corporate farming has now become an issue. I was once told, "75% of the Amish farm." This is no longer true. Large families and growing children who were once looking for

*See bibliography
** Part III "Amish and the English" *The Amish* of *Harmony* by Drucilla Milne, pages 108-109

land are now settling for a trade. It is much more profitable and attainable.

In 1974 when the Amish first moved here land prices were reasonable, (approximately $300 to $700 / acre). In 2007 land prices have gone higher and higher, (approximately $2000 to $3,500 / acre).

Small acre farms are not as available anymore, and more homes are being built on the farms the Amish do own. On one farm, for example, five homes have been built to house the grandparents, parents and two sons and one daughter.

It has been 20 or more years since guided car tours began. The tours of 1986 and 1987 were too numerous to count. People came by the bus loads. Those early tours only stopped at three or four Amish homes. I remember when Vernon asked me if I was interested in giving tours. I did not give my answer immediately. As I stated previously in the introduction, I was concerned how my Amish friends and neighbors would feel, so I asked them. They did not say yes or no. I was told, instead, "Rather you than someone else."

Amish tours continue to be popular. People in Harmony, Lanesboro, Mabel, Canton and Preston are or once were involved in providing Amish tours.

No matter where the Amish settle, they seem to draw attention to themselves and their simple lifestyle. Life in modern society can be confusing, complicated and hold too many entrapments. In giving tours, I often hear the longing that people have for what has been lost concerning a simpler life of years past.

Which reminds me once again of the remark Old Bishop Jake made referring to progress: "Progress is like falling off a roof. You can't stop the fall anymore than you can stop progress."

It is now a familiar sight to see cars, vans, and buses traveling through the Amish countryside. Newspapers, magazines, kings, queens, dignitaries and visitors from many countries and from all over the United States and all walks of life have taken an interest in the Amish way of life. Tourism has definitely cut into their simple lifestyle.

Part III

Amish Schools

State Laws and Amish Schools

Interviews With Teachers

Christmas in a One-Room
Schoolhouse

Old Order Amish Schools

Many Amish groups still use one-room schoolhouses. In the Harmony/Canton area there are ten such schools. These schools are placed within a reasonable radius, making them accessible to children living on Amish farms. The names of schools are often descriptive of the area were they are, such as Lenora Valley which is located near the small town of Lenora, Minnesota. They also take on a name of a once established one-room school of long ago, such as Scotland or Wilton Center Schools. More commonly the name is from a distinguishing characteristic of the land—Valley View, Crab Apple, and Meadow Valley Schools. Vale School in Canton Township was the first school, founded in 1974; the most recent school established was Meadow Valley School, which opened in Canton Township in 2001. At the time of this writing, only one family has had to use home schooling because they were too far from any of the existing Amish schools.

Advanced education is not valued in the Amish culture. In fact common sense is many times given more value than knowledge. Specifically, their education consists of an eighth grade elementary education. The four" R's" are taught—- reading, 'riting', 'rithmetic' and Respect.

The Amish speak Low German (also called Pennsylvania Dutch.) Little children who are under school age understand only Low German; English is taught after children enter school at the age of six. On Fridays, all lessons are taught in German. Schools have had as few as nine scholars and/or as many as forty. The one-room school having forty pupils had two teachers.

Each school has a school board made up of members from the local school district. When a school board recruits a teacher, she or he is an unmarried member of the Amish community. Teachers have no formal education and are not certified. Amish teachers are eighth grade educated and are termed 'easy learners', (good students) whom the community feels will make a good teacher. Teachers have been as young as sixteen but are generally older. Oftentimes an 'easy learner' has been a teacher's helper and is therefore comfortable with the schedule, material and students. If teachers do not live in the district where they are teaching, they will live with a local family who provides them with room and board.

Most of the teaching materials for the Amish schools come from

Ontario, Canada, or Ohio. They also use readers that the English schools used back in the 1930's and 1940's. These are the books featuring Dick, Jane, and Sally, Spot, their dog and Puff, their cat.

Examples of readers used are: *Our Heritage,* which is part of the Pathway Reading Series published by Pathway Publishing Corp. of Aylmer, Ohio, and LaGrange, Indiana. Titles of other books in the series are: *Thinking of Others* — Fifth grade; *Step by Step* — Sixth grade and *Seeking True Values* — Seventh grade. *Our Heritage* is the eighth grade textbook. *Our Heritage* contents are:

Unit One — *Our Heritage*
Unit Two — *True Values*
Unit Three — *People Who Serve*
Unit Four —- *Thinking of Others*
Unit Five — *Nature's Wonders*
Unit Six — *In Olden Days*
Unit Seven — *The Way of Love*
Unit Eight — *Home on the Farm*

Each unit begins with a Bible verse. For example, Unit One's Bible verse is Psalms 61:5. . . "Thou hast given me the heritage of those that fear thy name." On the following page is the poem "Our Help in Ages Past" by Isaac Watts:

"O God, our help in ages past,
Our hope for years to come,
Our shelter from the stormy blast
And our eternal home..."

A story "Church in the Pasture" follows the poem. The story combines reading skills with a history of the Amish experience. The preface states: "Because of persecution, our Anabaptist forefathers often met at night for religious services— in fields or barns or in the deep forest." The following story is about such a meeting which occurred "in a field just outside Leeuwarden (The Netherlands) in 1542." It is an adaptation of Chapter 13 of the book, *The Drummer's Wife:* "One of the speakers at this nighttime meeting was Menno Simons, whose biography 'One Hundred Guilders for Menno' you will find in a later unit of this book."

The story is followed by Thinking-It-Over questions and Word Study which includes *tremble, amble, reverberate, lot, alien, conspire, asunder, villain, traitor.*

The Blackboard Bulletin is a monthly magazine published by

Pathway Publishers. Teachers enjoy subscribing to this magazine, since most articles are written by scholars, teachers, school board members, and parents. These articles give advice, solution for discipline concerns, craft ideas, and much more.

State Law and Amish Schools

Although the Amish take no state aid, they do pay taxes, including school tax levies. The State does mandate that the Amish meet certain requirements concerning education. These include: 1.) Keeping attendance records 2.) Students must attend the required 170 days of school 3.) Students must attend the required number of hours each school day 4.) School must teach the basic skills 5.) Teachers must follow health and safety standards: however, immunizations are not required 6.) Students must attend school through the eighth grade.*

* Minnesota Department of Education, *Education Laws*, Vol. 1, Chapters 117-125, January, 1992

Old Order Amish Schools
(Minnesota)

There are ten one-room Amish schools in the Harmony-Canton-Mabel area:

1. *Vale School—Canton Township—Date founded—1974*
2. *Wilton Center School—Harmony Township—Date founded—1976*
3. *Scotland School—Preston Township—Date founded—1980*
4. *Grubb Hills School—Canton Township—Date founded—1984*
5. *Valley View School—Mabel Township—Date founded—1985*
6. *Du Shee Knob School—Canton Township—Date founded—1995*
7. *Crab Apple School—Amherst Township—Date founded—1989*
8. *Lenora Valley School—Lenora Township—Date founded—1992*
9. *Central View School—Harmony Township—Date founded—1993*
10. *Meadow Valley School—Canton Township—Date founded—2001*

Grubb Hills School

Starting the School Year
Grubb Hills School

Mattie has been hard to track down for an interview. I had driven to her home on two other occasions, but each time she was visiting at a sister's home. Today, she is at the home of yet another of her sisters, cleaning the house because Sunday church[3] is to be held in their home. As I pull into the yard, I see two small children playing in a black buggy. It is not hitched up. A little boy slowly approaches me, a

---

3 There are six church districts. When three have church, the other three church districts have a visiting Sunday. It switches on the following Sunday, three church districts have church while the other three have a visiting Sunday.

dog begins to bark and a woman surrounded by three more children appears in the doorway of the summer kitchen.[4]

"Is Mattie, the school teacher, here?" I ask. At about this same time, Mattie steps from the house onto the open porch. I introduce myself and ask if she would like me to share some of the interviews I've had with other teachers. A bench and small table are on the porch. We settle onto the bench. After reading some of my writings, we begin talking and I find out that she was eighteen when she began teaching, a typical age for an Amish school teacher.

How Mattie started teaching is a little different. She tells me, "The teacher at Grubb Hills School had twenty-six pupils and needed help. She asked if I would come on Tuesdays and Thursdays. That was my first year. The following year, I taught the full year and I had twenty-six pupils again. The third year, I had twelve pupils and no first graders. That was nice because they are the ones that need the most attention."

Curious about the custodial care of the schoolhouses, I ask Mattie how the cleaning gets done before the school year begins. "We have a cleaning day before school starts," Mattie replies. "The children help to get the school clean by washing windows, desks, and floors. The men help that day, too. The school lawn is left to grow all summer, so the men take a hay mower and cut the grass. They also do the bigger repairs."

Mattie tells me all the painting both outside and inside is done by the girls.

I say to Mattie, "I read in *The Blackboard Bulletin* that sometimes parents help with posters and doing other small tasks that help lighten a teacher's load. Have you found this to be true?"

"I had my cousins help me the first full year I taught. They helped me make posters. I do sometimes get advice from parents. Suggestions are given both ways."

Mattie tells me that older pupils often help the younger ones. "I had four eighth grade girls who took turns helping me. At the end of the year I gave them each a 'Berry Set' —that's a fruit bowl with six serving dishes to match. It was a gift for helping me."

I ask her if she has anything else she'd like to share with me.

"I wrote something in a poem about each of my twelve pupils last year. Would you like to see it?" I say that I would. I could not, however,

---

4 A summer kitchen is separate from the main house and is used for canning, butchering, laundry, etc. It keeps the heat out of the main kitchen in the hotter seasons of the year. It also keeps the main kitchen neat and orderly.

print the poem because she used her scholars full names. The Amish do not like to be singled out and I'd been told many times not to use proper names. From her poem, I could tell that Mattie has the qualities of a good teacher. The poem was cleverly constructed, giving praise to each one of her pupils.

Meadow Valley School

A Typical Amish School Day
Meadow Valley School

The Meadow Valley School teacher, Lovina, arrives early by horse and buggy. Before teaching at Meadow Valley, she taught at the Scotland School in Preston Township. In all, she has been teaching for eleven years.

She has chores to do before the children begin to arrive. One of these is to build a fire in the wood burning stove to warm the schoolroom. The children like to play outside until school starts. Before joining the boys who are playing in the schoolyard, the girls come into the schoolhouse and remove their bonnets. Leaving their prayer kapps and capes on, they go back outside to play. When it is time to start classes, the teacher rings a small bell, calling the children into the school. After hanging their jackets, capes, and straw hats in the entryway, the students go to their assigned desks.

Each morning begins with twenty minutes of singing. Two pupils lead the singing and at least two songs are sung. There is no musical accompaniment, only the sound of the children's voices raised in song.

The first class of the day is a language class. This is for all eight

25

grades. Some classes are given writing lessons, others have spelling lessons, and still others memorize a poem or verse or have reading assignments. Each class, as they are being taught, comes to a bench that has been placed beside the teacher's desk. While she is teaching one particular class, the other pupils are given assignments. There is a large blackboard on the wall behind her. In this school there are twenty-one students.

First graders learn the alphabet and the sounds of the letters via flashcards. These first graders learn their lessons both in English and in German. This is because, up to this point in their lives, they have known only Low German, so this is the language they know well. The teacher makes worksheets for the first graders; however, second grade through eighth grade have textbooks and workbooks for English and spelling.

After reading classes are finished, the children have a fifteen-minute recess before arithmetic class begins. There is then a one-hour lunch break, which includes playtime. Teachers usually go outside and join in the activities during this break. When I ask Lovina about students staying in during recess time to make up lessons or for disciplinary purposes, she replies, "I don't like to stay in any more than the pupils do, but sometimes it's necessary." The teacher also tells me about one student who forgot his lunch one day. Rather than seeing him go without lunch, she allowed him to drive her horse and buggy the two miles home while the other students were in their first class.

The afternoon lesson concentrates on English, after which the students are allowed to pursue individual activities. Sometimes they may write letters to someone who is ill or absent, or they might draw or color pictures. Another popular activity is doing "brain teasers," such as crossword puzzles or "Find the Word" sheets.

Spelling is the last class of the day. If time is left before dismissal, work is done using flashcards for numbers, ABC's, spelling, vocabulary or arithmetic. One row at a time in orderly fashion, the teacher dismisses the students. They go to the entryway to retrieve their jackets, capes, hats and bonnets, and gather in groups for their walks home.

Scotland School

Observation of an Amish Schoolroom
Scotland School

It is a cloudy day but the temperatures are mild, in the low 40s. As I leave my car, I see that the children are on their lunch break. They are standing in a muddy yard, throwing a ball over the schoolhouse to a group of children waiting on the other side. The game is "Annie, Annie Over." [5]

"Is your teacher here?" I call as I approach the school.

A student replies, "Yes. She's here!" Among the crowd of children, I then see a small-framed woman with brown eyes wearing wire rimmed glasses. As all the teachers do, she is in the schoolyard, playing the game with the children. When she sees me, she leaves the children and walks towards me. I notice the schoolyard is very muddy, and there is mud spattered on the walls and the door and windows of the school.

I gesture towards all the mud and ask, "What happened here?"

"A truck backed up to the windows and door of the school and spun its wheels, spattering mud all over. The students and I will have to do some cleaning." I assume this was done as a nasty prank; no more is said about the act by either of us.

She tells me this is her first year teaching. She started when she was seventeen. She has twenty-four scholars. Seven of her students were in school when she was. She is also teaching thirteen of her cousins.

---

5 One child calls out "Annie-Annie Over" and throws the ball over the building to the children on the other side. If they catch the ball they can sneak around the building and throw the ball at the children on the other side or catch them and tag them.

As we enter the schoolroom, I see a large blackboard with an assignment written on it. She tells me it is a lesson for her older scholars.

"Are the students grouped by ability as well as by age?" I ask.

"No," she replies. "That would be too confusing for me."

I wonder if those scholars who have an interest and the ability to learn more quickly listen to the upper classes and absorb the lessons the other scholars are given. She replies, "I remember doing that."

The room is cheerful and has many motivating posters which encourage the scholars to strive for excellence. On one wall there are three readings:

WELCOME:
W— Wear a smile
E—Enter into discussions.
L—Listen to instructions carefully.
C--Cooperate with others.
O—Open your books carefully.
M—Make sure lessons are always done on time
E—Enjoy the school year.

School:
S - Study
C - Courage
H - Honesty
0 – Obedience
0 - Organized
L - Love

The Grammar in Rhyme
A noun is a name of anything,
As school or garden, hoop, ring.
Adjectives tell what kind of noun,
Great, small. Pretty. White or brown.
Instead of a noun, a pronoun stands,
For John's head, his face, my hand.
Verbs tell of something being done,
To read, write, sing, spell, or run.
Before the noun a preposition stands,
To the church, from a tree, on his land.
"I connect" the conjunction says,
Sentences and words, tomorrow or today.
How things are done the adverb tells,
As slowly, quickly, ill, or well.
They also tell us where or when,
As here, there, now, and then.
Interjections show surprise,
"Oh" how pretty and "Oh" how wise.

Near the teacher's desk is a chart with each student's name on one line and stars placed after the student's name. The star system rewards the students for lessons completed and motivates them to do well. It is evident from the number of stars behind the students' names that they are learning.

As a former Amish teacher who is now a buggy maker told me, the talent and skills the students have are not displayed by the star system alone. Many times schoolroom education does not show a child's real talents. These normally don't come into view until after their eighth grade education is completed. It is then that these young people can choose to apprentice in particular areas. Some of these areas are blacksmithing, wood crafting, becoming wheelwrights, harness and bridle making, farming, carpentering, repairing the community's diesel and gas engines, and many other pursuits.

Valley View School

The Importance of Reading and Books
Valley View School

On this summer's day, the mid-afternoon is very hot. The windows and doors of the teacher's home are open to catch any stray breeze that might come along. As I walk up to the house and onto the open porch of the home, a young Amish woman comes to the door to greet me. Caroline is expecting me, since I had been here last week. Although she was in South Dakota on that day, I had told her family that I would be back soon.

The intensity of the day's heat is matched by the heat coming from the kitchen. "I've been canning peaches," Caroline explains. "It's too hot in the kitchen. I'll get some chairs and we can sit out here on the porch." We settle ourselves by a table on one side of the porch.

Caroline has been teaching for twelve years and began teaching at the age of twenty. She says, "I remember that you stopped at Scotland School one day when I was teaching there." Her statement reminds me that I had been there borrowing books when she was teaching.

"The largest class I had was twenty-six pupils at Scotland School. My smallest class was eleven, but then a family moved, so I had only eight for the remainder of that year. This fall, I'll have eighteen."

"What do you think you stress the most when you're teaching?" I ask.

"I like to teach the sounds at the same time I'm teaching the alphabet," she responds. "If the students understand both sounds and the ABC's they can read much faster and better."

The Amish classrooms that I have been in have all had posters to encourage student learning. When I ask if she has any other special posters for her students, she tells me, "Yes, I have the 'Golden Rule'— "You shall love your neighbor as yourself."

"Is there anything that comes to your mind about teaching any particular students? I don't want names, only the memory you carry with you."

"I had two brothers," she begins. "One was always looking out the window, and I thought he was a slow-learner. His brother was a fast-learner. This went on for a year or so. Then their roles switched. The slow-learner became the better student, and his brother became the one who looked out the window all the time."

"What are they doing now?" I ask.

"The one who looked out the window all the time at first is farming. The other one is making furniture."

"I have one last question. What do you enjoy most about teaching?"

Without hesitating, she replies, "I enjoy the children and books."

This teacher's sensitivity and her experience during the last twelve years have contributed to her being a good teacher. It is an added bonus that she enjoys the children and books.

Vale School, newly built.

A Family of Teachers
Vale School

When this young Amish teacher sees me approach the house, she steps outside into a small breeze-way. We stay in this area where there is a cool breeze. A blue cupboard gives me something to write on as I take my notes.

During the course of our conversation, I find out she is nineteen and in her third year of teaching. She had previously substituted for a former teacher whenever she was needed. Two of her five sisters were also teachers.

"What was the first school that you taught in and how many students did you have?" I ask.

"It was Vale School; I had twenty-six pupils."

"That is a lot of students for a first year teacher," I comment. "What do you do to make the lessons more enjoyable for your students?"

"I get them involved as much as I can to keep them interested in the subjects I'm teaching." Her expressive brown eyes light up as she explains." There are lesson exercises we do. We often play guessing games that have to do with their reading lesson. I ask them what they think is going to happen in our next story."

"The days can be very different," she continues. "A day might start out slowly but be stimulated by the enthusiasm of the children and their good humor. That can be reversed, too. I may come into the classroom with enthusiasm when the children need a boost and I energize them."

A younger sister and three of her six brothers are still in school. They ride with her in the buggy to school, where they are in her classroom.

She is typical of the teachers who enjoy their pupils and take their

31

positions seriously. This family has been active in teaching young minds, using their own talents to further the children's education.

Crab Apple School

A Teacher's Stories
Crab Apple School

As I drive by the green woods and fields of the Amish settlement, I see the damage from the rain and wind storm that hit the night before. Several branches and leaves lie on the road. A tree is uprooted in one yard. The storm has made the temperatures a little cooler after the rain.

Driving up the gravel road to the home, I see a black buggy in the yard. The occupants—a woman and child—-are visiting with the mother who lives here, while some of her children stand around her. They range from very young to about fourteen years of age. I roll down my window and ask for Ruth, the daughter who is a school teacher. They finish visiting and Ruth's mother invites me into her home. This family consists of nine girls and two boys. Two of the girls are busy preparing the noon meal.

Typical of Amish homes, the floors are bare and the curtains are navy blue and attached to the window frame with a loop on a hook or nail. (There are no curtain rods).There is a calendar on one wall, but no pictures or wall decorations of any other kind. A few dishes made of colored glass are displayed on the tops of hutches or on shelves.

After being introduced to Ruth, I ask her if we can go into the larger room, where we can visit uninterrupted. It takes only a little encouragement to get Ruth's mother to join us. She is concerned as to what questions I will ask her daughter.

Ruth appears to be quiet by nature, so to draw her out, I decide to read her a few interviews I've had with other teachers. This will also give her an idea as to what others have shared. I read a newspaper article I wrote about Christmas in a one-room Amish schoolhouse. Both Ruth and her mother begin guessing who the teacher featured in the article might be. It is fun and as we share this time together we become more relaxed and comfortable with each other.

The first question I ask Ruth is, "How old were you when you began teaching?" I know that oftentimes the teachers are selected from among the young women who were good students as they went through their eight years of schooling. I am not surprised, therefore, when Ruth replies, "I was seventeen, but before the year was over I was eighteen."

In our area, there are ten one-room Amish schoolhouses where Grades 1-8 are taught. Wondering about the typical number of students in a school, I inquire how many students Ruth had the previous year.

"I had nine students—eight boys and one girl," Ruth answers.

"Did you have someone in all eight grades?"

"No," Ruth responds. "I didn't have any students in second grade or fourth grade."

When I ask her where she stayed during the week when she was teaching, Ruth's mother speaks up. "She preferred coming home every night. She even insulated her buggy with double bubble-wrap and put it on the floor of the buggy. Some people use this same type of insulation for the buggy roofs, too."

Ruth's drive to school was about six miles, and the insulation made the ride in the cold Minnesota winter more comfortable. Ruth's schedule was to leave home at 7:00 AM, with school starting at 9:00 AM.

Just before I leave, I ask her if she has anything else that she would like to share with me. To my pleasant surprise, she says, "I'll write you a story and send it to you." I ask her if it is a true story about her classroom, to which she answers, "Yes."

I enjoyed my visit with Ruth, as well as with the other teachers. She impressed me with her thoughtfulness and desire to be a good teacher. The qualities she possesses will be passed on to her "scholars," as the Amish call the students.

A few days later, I received Ruth's story in the mail. It was carefully written out in longhand. The story is given below:

"The Vacuum Cleaner Box"

The hay was put into the empty vacuum cleaner box so I could feed my horse at school. I arrived around 7:35 AM, and then fed my horse the hay I'd brought with me. I smiled as I took the hay from the re-used vacuum cleaner box, remembering the rabbit dad had brought home in it for the younger children last week.

As I entered the one-room schoolhouse, I saw sand on the floor. The children had been playing in the sand pile and sand was everywhere. I swept and mopped the floor quickly before the children arrived.

Sometime during the school day, they discovered the vacuum cleaner box. They assumed I had a battery-operated vacuum cleaner. (The Amish would not use such a modern, electrical or battery operated apparatus.) Since they didn't see it, they thought I had hidden it. Unbeknown to me, the boys looked all that week for the vacuum cleaner. They even told the younger boys to ask to see my vacuum cleaner. When these boys came into the schoolhouse to ask, I could not understand what they were talking about.

On Fridays, we have a cleaning day. I told my eight boys they could go outside and play while the one girl, Becky, and I did the cleaning. Normally the boys help, too, but on this day I didn't think it was necessary. The two oldest boys went to the nearest farm and got hot water for cleaning.

Meanwhile, the other boys decided the only place they hadn't looked for this vacuum cleaner was in the attic of the schoolhouse. (I didn't even realize there was an attic!)

They made a plan to get me out of the school so they could look in the attic. They all got sticks and began banging on the open door and the side of the schoolhouse. If I didn't have a headache then, I knew I would soon have one with all that commotion going on.

I took the gallon pail of dirty water we'd been cleaning with and, before I even realized what I was doing, I threw the water out the open door and onto them. "Enough is enough!" I said.

They were taken so by surprise that they just stood there, sticks in hands, with a shocked look on all their faces. I had to turn quickly and go into the school because I couldn't hold my laughter.

I found out later from one of the mothers that they thought I had hidden the vacuum cleaner in the school.

The children and I have had many a good laugh over that vacuum cleaner box!

Another story Ruth related to me about her class involved Valentine's Day:

A Valentine's Story
(Note: Crab Apple School had eight boys and one girl.)

Valentine's Day is just like any other day, except we have a little extra fun by making valentines and exchanging names for valentines and lunchboxes. Whoever picks your name gets your lunch box and a valentine. The lunch boxes are packed with special care on this day. The extra treat may be something like gum, candy or potato chips.

After lunch, the children exchange valentines.

I made one valentine for each of the pupils. I gave them their valentines and didn't get any except from the only girl, Becky. I didn't mind, but I could see that the boys were ashamed that they didn't have any valentines to give me.

They sat looking at each other but didn't know what to do or say. The oldest boy hurriedly made me a valentine, and the others quickly did the same, except for the youngest, a first grader.

I had to laugh when I saw the boys' funny valentines. They had drawn everything from Christmas trees to dogs, horses, hammers and saws. I thought it was fun and appreciated them all.

Written by Ruth, teacher of Crab Apple School

Wilton Center School

Grandma Mattie and the Teachers' Prayer Kapps
Wilton Center

Grandma Mattie lives in the 'Grossdadi' house, a home added for parents when a married child takes over the farm. Mattie's is located near the home where the school teacher I am going to interview lives with her parents and siblings. We made plans to meet at Grandma Mattie's home because we thought she would enjoy the company.

I am the first to arrive at Grandma's home. The main door is open and a nice breeze is coming in the screened door. I knock and call out, "Mattie, are you home?"

"Drucie, come in and sit down. It's been a long time since you've been by."

When I enter the main room of the home, I see she is sitting with her feet soaking in a pan of water on the floor in front of her chair.

"I've been having some trouble with my feet swelling," she explains. "It helps to soak them in water." For a short time, we discuss her health, the weather, and the jars of canned apple sauce and apple butter that sit on the table. Soon her granddaughters arrive, both have been teachers.

Almost immediately, Grandma says something to the youngest in Pennsylvania Dutch. Obviously following the instructions she has been given, Mattie's granddaughter picks up a pair of black stockings from the floor and takes them into a connecting bedroom.

"Don't worry about how your house looks," I tease Grandma Mattie. "It's so clean we could eat off the floors." This brings laughter and more teasing over her unnecessary concern.

"The girls keep house for me," Grandma Mattie says—just like her to give credit where credit is due.

Our conversation turns to schools and the girls' love for teaching. The older of the two has enjoyed being a teacher for three years at Lenora Valley School. Before she began teaching at twenty-one, she had made baskets for her aunt and uncle at their craft shop. She enjoyed this job but was anxious for the chance to teach.

I ask her, "Do you wear a white prayer kapp when you teach?" A white prayer kapp[6] is heavily starched and pinched into tiny pleats that must be ironed in with a heavy cast iron that is heated on a wood burning stove.

"Yes, I do, "she replies. "And the girls who are pupils wear black prayer kapps." Black kapps are more practical for small girls and young girls because they don't show the soiling and they don't have to be pleated.

Grandma Mattie speaks up, with a twinkle in her eye, "She wears a white one so the scholars can see who the boss is."

I turn to Sara, who also teaches, and tell her, "I went by your school one afternoon and saw you sitting on the back step. Your hair was down and you were getting it pinned up to put under your prayer kapp."

"Yes," she laughs. "My hair had come loose. The girls were watching me and ran away with some of my hairpins. They love to tease me."

The windows are open and, as we talk, dusk sets in. Grandma Mattie tells the girls to light the kerosene lamp. The mellow light reflects off the white walls, the oak floors and furniture.

We hear younger sisters playing and laughing out in the yard. The girls become quiet, and then there is soft whispering outside Grandma's windows. One sister peeks in the window and quickly disappears. Another sister whispers to teacher Mattie through the open window and they laugh together as if sharing a private joke. The girls are having fun teasing us.

Soon it is time for me to leave. Teacher Mattie will stay with her Grandmother this night to help her and see to her comfort. It has been an evening of fun and company for Grandmother Mattie.

Lenora Valley School

6   On church Sundays, young single girls wear a black prayer kapp to church and those who are married, widowed or older wear a white prayer kapp.

Grubb Hills School. Notice the wheel chair ramp.

Teaching and Compassion
Grubb Hills and Du Shee Knob

I have an appointment to interview two teachers who are sisters. Their nine-year-old brother Enos was in an accident while helping his brother saw wood. They were using a buzz saw hooked to a gas motor. Enos' jacket was caught in the drive shaft. As the shaft turned, the jacket twisted and pulled Enos into the rotating shaft. The engine shut down immediately, but Enos was still severely injured. I am hoping to find out how he is doing as well.

When I arrive at the family's home on a hill, the father is unhitching the horse from the buggy. Two of the smaller children come down the hill to meet me. The older girl speaks English, but the young boy is not yet in school, so he speaks only Low German. They lead me up the steps to the large, open porch. The smell of good food cooking drifts out of the kitchen, where there is much activity.

The women are busy cleaning and preparing food for the upcoming wedding of a neighbor girl. She is to be married on Thursday; Amish weddings are held October through March on either a Tuesday or a Thursday. Usually, when there is a wedding, it is held in the home of the bride and the reception is held in a home nearby. This is so the food preparation can continue while the wedding is being held. The meal is then ready to serve the guests after the wedding. (All church activities are held in Amish homes because there are no church buildings.)

Just inside the door, Enos is sitting in his wheelchair. I am struck by what a handsome young boy he is. His black hair has a dark scarf tied over it. His eyelashes are dark and long. A hard brace is on his right arm, while his legs are in Styrofoam braces, held closed with Velcro. When I speak to him, he is shy and ducks his head to one side, avoiding my eyes.

Du Shee Knob School

Ironically, another nine-year-old named Enos was also in an accident.* I had written an article about these two boys, and when I ask Enos, "Do you want to hear what I've written about you and your friend?" he overcomes his shyness long enough to nod his head. After I'm done reading, we discuss Enos's care and progress. He is being given physical therapy treatments in a small town nearby.

The girls, however, are anxious to get to their interviews as school teachers. I begin with the older of the two, who has taught for two years at Du Shee Knob School. She tells me that she is in her second year of fulltime teaching. Before that, she began teaching when she substituted for a cousin who went to her brother's wedding.

"How many students did you have when you started teaching?"

"I had eleven both years and the same students. It was easier for me the second year because I knew what my pupils were capable of."

* Part VIII: Other Stories- "Accidents"

We discuss how the teachers get their supplies. She tells me the teachers make a list of what they need and the treasurer of the school board then gets the supplies.

"What did you do for Christmas those years?" I ask.

It does not surprise me to hear of her compassion when she replies, "We didn't exchange gifts because one family had six children in my classroom, and I thought it would be too much for them to buy that many gifts."

The younger sister Emma tells me that she began teaching when the teacher at Crab Apple School left in the middle of the year. Hearing this, her mother adds, "My brother who was on the school board thought Emma should teach. She was fifteen and one half—she should really have been older—but they were desperate for a teacher. The school had gone two weeks without a teacher. They had asked many girls, but no one wanted the job."

"And I always wanted to be a teacher," Emma interjects. "I had fifteen students that first year. I remembered how I was taught and just started."

I had been told that school boards, who are made up of parents from the area where the schools are located, will step in if there are behavior problems with students, so I ask her, "Did you have any problems with discipline?"

"No," she replies.

Emma has just finished her third year of teaching. Recently, she taught at the Grubb Hills School. "I had my brother Enos in school after his accident," she tells me. "He wouldn't have been able to return had I not been the teacher. I also had to help him with his care. He sat in the back of the room with our sister, who is twelve-years-old. She helped him with his studies."

"What did his care consist of?"

"He has a hole where his tracheotomy was, and it needs suctioning sometimes. He also needs help when he has to cough." Emma goes on to say that her brother also has a catheter in his bladder and the bag sometimes needs emptying.

At this point, the father asks if I'd ever seen where a tracheotomy tube is put. He proceeds to remove the gauze from his son's throat to show me. He also shows me the suction device Enos needs, which is in a cloth bag at the back of his wheelchair.

Three times while I am there, Enos looks as if he is choking; however, he is just trying to cough. Each time, his father gets up and presses Enos's diaphragm to force air into his lungs to help him cough.

The care and attention Enos receives from his family is heartwarming to see.

Just as the girls are compassionate teachers who are committed to their students, so is the concern for their young brother commendable. Emma, who was barely eighteen, accepted the responsibility both as his sister and as his teacher quite willingly.

Only a few months after my visit, Enos was able to go fishing with some family members and friends. He was able to enjoy the day and also caught fish.

Central View Schools

Amish School Boards
Central View School

It is a hot Friday afternoon and the temperature has reached 91 degrees. When I enter the yard of this homestead, I see a small shed with a porch attached displaying crafts for sale. Dark clothes hang on the clothesline, drying in the warm air. Near the house is a large garden with flowers and vegetables. At the door of the home, the mother and younger daughter peer out at me. The mother comes out to greet me as I approach and then ushers me into their home.

The family has just finished eating their noon meal and the girls are starting to clear the long harvest table. Five boys sit on the long benches at the side of the table. When they finish their meal, they go outside to rest in the shade of the trees. Lovina, the teacher I have come to interview, finds a chair for me and invites me to sit with her. When the table is cleared, her two sisters begin washing the dishes.

At the age of twenty, Lovina has just finished her first year of teaching. "My friend who had been teaching at the Lenora Valley School for the past three years had wanted to request a transfer to

41

Central View School," she recalls. "Then this spring, she was asked to bake for a farmer's market bake shop. She decided she didn't want to take the position away from me and, instead of teaching, began working in the bake shop. Her wages would have been more than mine since she had three years of experience. I always wanted to teach and was happy for the opportunity."

"How do you get paid?" I ask. "By the month? Or does it depend on how many scholars you have or how many years you've been teaching?"

"A teacher over twenty-years-old gets more than those who are under twenty. It doesn't go by the number of pupils. Those who have taught longer probably get more. I will get $25 to $30 more this year."

"I'm interested in knowing more about your school boards. How many are on a school board?"

"There are three members; each one is on for three years. One goes off each year and is replaced"

"Are these men voted on?"

"Yes. We have a meeting one week before school starts. We replace the one board member going off."

She goes on to explain, "The position of the school treasurer is separate and not held by a school board member. When I need paper for the duplicator and other things, I buy the supplies and turn in the bill to the treasurer, who pays me back." From talking with other Amish teachers, I know that they sometimes buy special treats such as stickers and small gifts with their own money as well.

"Do all the families in the school district, whether they are single, widowed, or grandparents, pay into the fund for school supplies?"

"I'm not sure about that, "she responds, "but I think everyone does."

As all the Amish teachers do, Lovina joins the children in playing games during their breaks. Her favorite game to play is softball, just as it is a favorite game with her pupils. A poem she wrote about her scholars reflects this:

End of the School Term
The end of the school term is near.
How can it be that it is already here?
Our favorite game was softball,
Both in the spring and the fall.
You worked your best,
When taking a test.
Now it is time to say good-bye.
Enjoy your summer,
And I hope it doesn't fly by.

Christmas in a One-Room Amish School

It was near the Christmas holiday and one of the Amish parents told me to go to the home of a teacher who had a unique idea for celebrating Christmas. The teacher was no longer teaching since she had gotten married the year before.

The school where she had taught is near the home where she now lives with her new husband. As I drive up the long lane and past the school, I notice how conveniently located the school is, close to many Amish homes.

This teacher's home is large with a porch that stretches across the front of the house. After we exchange greetings, she invites me into her home. I tell her that one of her neighbors suggested I talk to her. She tells me a little background on her teaching experience. She was eighteen when she began teaching so her wages went to help supplement her parents' and siblings' living expenses. However, when she came of age and was planning to be married, she began saving for her own marital living expenses. She enjoyed teaching for six years. Her students ranged from first grade, six years old, to eighth grade, thirteen to fourteen years old.

After I ask several questions about Christmas at the Amish schools, she describes how she celebrated Christmas with the students in her classroom:

"Christmas is celebrated on the day that is closest to December 25th, since there is never school on the 25th. We have some lessons but it is a lighter teaching day. School is let out an hour to 45 minutes early."

"People of the community thought it would be better for the children to exchange food rather than gifts because it would be more fair and affordable. I told the children that we would be exchanging lunch boxes. (Children carry a cold meal in a black metal lunch bucket to school.) I sent notes home with the children so parents would be aware of our plan."

"Parents took special care in packing the children's lunches that day. They packed hot dogs, pizza, pretzels, pudding, peanuts, pie, cookies, cake, and other good food for the children. There was great excitement as lunchtime approached."

"After the lunch exchange, we played games. I call one game we played 'The Fun Box'. We played the game this way: I divided the children into pairs and had each pair write on a piece of paper what they would like to do as a fun activity. Some suggestions were: piecing a puzzle together, coloring, writing on the blackboard or drawing a picture, singing a song or reciting a nursery rhyme. You would be surprised at some of the suggestions. One young pair of boys suggested going outside and running around the schoolhouse one time." She laughs when she says this. "The children had fun and so did I."

"I gave an orange or apple and a small gift to each of my pupils. I gave many different gifts over the six years I taught. Some of the gifts were jacks, stencils with numbers and letters, hammers, balls, compasses, beads, small dishes. They were usually inexpensive gifts that I could afford."

As she is finishing her description I ask, "Did you receive gifts?"

I am surprised and pleased when she begins to bring out of the cupboards—seemingly from every nook and cranny—gifts given to her by appreciative parents of the past six years. She remembers who gave her each gift. Her harvest table is soon laden with these gifts which include: towels, dishcloths, a recipe book, serviceable and pretty dishes, plastic covered containers, a sewing kit and many more items. There is also material from which she made a bright burgundy dress. She describes it as, "A most precious gift of material."

"People were generous to me, and most of the time their gifts had fruit, nuts, or candy accompanying them."

Amish children don't have a Christmas vacation. Schools are let out only for work related events such as the week during corn husking time (families pick and husk corn by hand together) and for religious holidays, such as Easter, Ascension Day, and Christmas Day.

In Amish homes, families get together throughout the Christmas season. Each separate family has its own holiday gathering, celebrating with prayer, food, candy and sometimes gifts. These gifts are simple and practical and may be either homemade or purchased.

Christmas is celebrated in the most simple and humble manner, without Christmas trees, wreaths or any other decorations. Their Christmas is celebrated on Jan. 6th, which they term the "Real Christmas" or "Old Christmas." It is the twelfth day after "our Christmas" (Dec. 25th). Since the actual date of Jesus' birth is unknown, it is Jan. 6th, Epiphany, that is observed as the feast of Jesus' baptism, with a secondary importance placed on His birth.

The Amish emphasize that gifts are not always tangible; there are gifts of love, just as God gave us His gift of love in the form of His son, Jesus.

Part IV

Apprenticeships and Jobs

Amish Apprenticeships and Jobs

The Amish are primarily a self-sustaining community. Although they work in the English world, they are still anchored in their own culture and strive to fill their basic needs through their own ingenuity and work, always keeping in mind the ways of their Old Order. This is the least progressive group of the Amish culture. The basic education they are taught is sufficient since they put more stress on farming and trades. These trades are learned through a system of apprenticeships, which offer "hands on" experience or they are self-taught. Advanced education is not valued in the Amish culture. They believe common sense has as much value as knowledge. Both are valued to get along in life.

Young people serve as apprentices in many occupations such as farmers, harness craftsmen, buggy builders, wheelwrights, farriers, blacksmiths, carpenters, furniture and window craftsmen, sawmill workers, sheet metal workers, masons, and construction builders. Some young men and women become teachers. Women learn to become caretakers and homemakers. Some of them also become midwives. They are taught crafts as well, which include making baskets and rugs, quilting, and woodworking.

Amish-made crafts for sale.

The Buggy Builder

When I arrive to visit Jonas, his wife tells me he is in his shop near the house. The sun has already gone down and there is very little natural light filtering into the windows of the shop. As I enter I call out, "Are you in here?" He responds and quickly lights a lamp for our comfort. It fills the area with a nice glow as I explain the reason for my visit. I notice the shop is uncluttered and there is only one buggy in a nearly completed state in one corner. On a previous visit he had two buggies in the shop. One was outside to be repaired.

Buggies are an essential part of the Old Order Amish lifestyle. Rather than dashing around in cars, the Amish have preserved the old-fashioned, slower way of traveling by horse and buggy. One Amish man used to joke about this and referred to his horse as an "oats mobile." He even went so far as to say the horse manure on the roads was "horse exhaust'.

In the Harmony-Canton area we had an Amish shop called Crossroad Buggies where these buggies were made. The owner moved to Missouri and sold the farm. A sawmill now exists on this farm.

There have been three men who have built the horse-drawn buggies for the Amish community: Henry, Andy and Jonas. The current buggy builder has not named his shop.

On our previous visit Jonas told me he'd never apprenticed with anyone. He took an interest in this buggy building and began learning the trade.

"Was there a lot to be learned?" I ask.

"I had worked with buggies some before starting to build them on my own. It was just something I was interested in doing."

I make the comment, "I believe we sometimes have talents that don't

An Amish buggy in the making.

necessarily show up until later in life. It doesn't necessarily need to be taught."

"My wife and I helped out teaching for one term," he responds. "We found that being an easy-learner or a slow-learner does not tell a child's worth."

We talk of schools and the fact that book learning does not always prove where the talents of a child lie. The star system might encourage a child to strive but the number of stars on a chart doesn't tell what the end results will be.

I tell him of one teacher's observation of two of her students—an easy-learner and a dreamer, who she thought was a slow-learner. Her notion proved to be wrong when the roles of these two children switched. The easy learner became the dreamer and the slow-learner became the easy-learner. Both young men are successful in their chosen occupations.

He says, "I was an easy-learner and enjoyed teaching. My wife and I both enjoyed the children and teaching." (His wife at this time is teaching a neighbor's Downs Syndrome child who is nine years old. She comes three times a week and they work and play together. The child already knows some of her letters and can tell the beginning letter of her siblings' names.)

Jonas and his wife are doing a service and have taken an interest in their community and the children in it.

"Have you had anyone apprentice with you?"

He replied, "No, it hasn't happened yet."

I asked, "Approximately how much does a buggy cost to build at this time?"

"The cost is around $1,500 but materials are going up all the time and I'll be raising the price next year."

The parts for buggies are ordered from Ohio and are trucked to his shop. He cuts the wood, bends the iron and does the upholstery work on the carriage seats. The axles are bought.

"I know when the Crossroad Buggy Shop was in business, there was a man of importance from Sudan who ordered and had a buggy shipped to his country. Have you made buggies for other states or countries?"

He laughs and replies, "Only to Arizona, and then a friend of his wanted a buggy also. I made two for the Dakotas, too." I asked who it was in Arizona and as it turns out, the man was from Harmony and a shirt-tail relative of my husband.

"I made three that went to Lamoni, Iowa, and some went up into northern Minnesota." They were picked up and delivered in a stock trailer. Usually someone is hired to do this.

He has about a dozen buggies on order at the time of this writing.

He and his wife are approaching their latter years of life; however, they both are enjoying these years. A son and his family live on the same building site and there is much activity to keep the cycle of life interesting and lively.

The Wheelwright

The Amish man walking from the barn to meet me is a wheelwright. His primary occupation is that of a farmer. He farms about sixty acres, as well as milking cows. At thirty-five years of age, he still has dark hair and a thick beard. He is the father of eleven children.

I introduce myself and ask, "Could I have fifteen minutes of your time? I'm writing a book and would like to visit with you about your wheelwright shop."

He, in turn, asks, "What kind of book are you writing?"

"I've talked to the ten teachers in the community this summer, " I respond, "and I would also like to write about apprenticeships and jobs available to young people in the Amish community. I will come back and let you read what I've written, before it goes into print."

My words seem to reassure him and he consents, "We can talk in the shop."

Entering his wheelwright shop I immediately see an impressive number of wheels leaning on one wall just inside the door of the shop. These are in different stages of completion. They are mostly of new wood, which is very stark looking, like newly stripped bark would appear. One stack has the spokes on the hub while the others are finished except for the steel band which needs to be added. Steel-banded wood wheels are essential to the Amish, as they use them on their buggies.

Wood wheels with steel bands around them for buggies.

"How did you get started making wheels?"

"A friend and I went to an Amish man over by Granger to ask questions and found out more about the trade. I opened my shop about four years ago. I order the parts and put them together."

"Are the tires shipped in the width needed?"

"That's right; I cut the tyre to length and size, it's spelled t-y-r-e.[7] I get the steel bands ready, and then take them to a welder."

"Is the wood steam-bent for the wheel?" I ask

"It's called felloe.[8] Yes, the felloe is steam-bent before it is sent to me. I order the spokes too. The felloe is sent in the right width and I measure it for the wheel."

I ask, "Could you make a living being a wheelwright?"

"No," he answers. "I couldn't do this for a living. The community here is too small, if it were bigger I could."

"So you really do this as a service for your community." He nods the affirmative.

7 The tyre is the steel band that is put on the felloe after the wheel is finished. It too is sent in the width needed.
8 Felloe is the wood rim of the wheel.

The community at one time ordered and bought the wheels in Ohio. This wheelwright's initiative and effort means that his fellow Amish no longer have to be dependent on an outside source. The wheel service that he offers in his shop makes it more convenient for the community.

A Farrier by Trade

One of this farrier's first statements catches my interest immediately. As a young boy, he began watching his father while he shoed the horses; "I almost stood underneath Dad. I wanted to get as close as I could."

He is a man now of twenty-nine years of age, and he has built up a business involving his interest in horses and their needs. People have brought their horses into his shop and then told others of their satisfaction with the way he handles the horses and does his work. I also learned of his trade and of him personally by 'word of mouth'.

When I turn my car onto the looped gravel driveway, I notice the 'Closed' sign posted in the shop window. There's no activity of any kind around the two metal, red sided buildings, nor around the house. I knock on the door going into the entry of the home. His wife comes into the entry and tells me he is sleeping. "He had an accident last night and hurt his hand."

"Let him sleep. I can come back another time."

"He's been sleeping for three hours and should probably get up anyway." I am hesitant to have her wake him, but she thinks it will be all right, so I tell her I will wait in the car.

When he comes out of the house, I see immediately that he is not feeling well. His index finger on his right hand has a large bandage on it and he is resting it on his left shoulder, holding it in position with his left hand. He sits in a small white child's wagon that is in the yard next to my car. He is very pale in appearance.

"You don't look like you feel well. I can come back later."

"Yah, I got my finger jammed while I was working with a horse last night between seven and eight o'clock. They took me to Rushford, then Winona, and then to Rochester to see a hand specialist. I didn't get home 'til this morning."

"I'm going; you look like you have a lot of pain." I could see he was getting whiter by the minute.

"They gave me something for that but it's wearing off. Come back next week."

When I return on the following Tuesday, everything is again quiet. I suspect he has returned to the doctor. I am met at the door by his wife, who tells me her husband and their seven-year-old boy have gone to town to run some errands. I ask her if she will show me where he had his accident and how it happened. We go into the shop and she tells me that her husband has crushed nerves in his finger and a chip out of a bone at the tip.

As his wife and I are visiting, we hear her husband returning from town. He and his wife exchange a few words in their Pennsylvania Dutch language, and then she goes to the house, taking her son with her. The farrier then pulls up a chair for me and we begin visiting. He tells me how the accident happened.

"It was getting dark, and I was just finishing up working on a draft horse. I should have taken the time to get a flashlight but I thought I could handle it." He made his mistake, when he went to unhook the apparatus which holds up the collared hoof. He should have released the hoof from the padded collar and let the horse's hoof down first. Suddenly the horse lurched forward, smashing the tip of his finger!

"The guy I was doing the work for took me to the doctor. He unhooked his truck from the trailer and took me first to Rushford, then to Winona, and there they told me I needed to see a hand specialist in Rochester, Minnesota. They gave me morphine, which took the edge off 'til I got help. I was lucky I didn't have to have surgery."

We talked more and then I ask, "How long have you had this shop?"

"I built it three years ago. I worked for another guy for three months. I mostly learned the shoeing and trimming on my own. I worked for my dad as a carpenter for one and one half years. I just worked shoeing on weekends at first. Dad said I could do this full-time if I wanted and work with him when I needed to."

Mules waiting for their hooves to be trimmed in the ferrier's shop

51

Anvil in the ferrier's shop.

"Can you make a living at this?"

"I did the horse shoeing and worked making buckboards and buggies in the winter for filler. I probably made two buggies a winter and did some repairs on others. I didn't live here then"

"How many new buggies and buckboards do you think you've made?"

"I've made about fifteen or twenty buggies and five new buckboards."

"About how many horses do you work on in a week's time?"

"I keep track of that just for my own records." He gets up from his chair and reaches into a cupboard for a notebook. "I did seventy a week for a while but I do more than that some weeks, about seventy-two to seventy-four. I have 'open' shoeing[9] on Mondays. I used to have 'open' shoeing two or three days a week but now only on Mondays. I've thought about putting up a print-out in the shop so people can see I shoe and trim between 930 and 940 horses in a year."

"How many horses can you get done in a normal day?"

"If I get started at six and work till seven-thirty I can do sixteen, that is probably two trims and the rest are shoed."

"Do you have some special techniques you use when working with horses?"

"Shoeing can be complicated. The problem can usually be fixed most of the time, if the horse is brought in more often, about every 6 to 8 weeks. I get the *Farrier's Journal.* I like that magazine and get a lot of good from it. I've gone to a convention for farriers in Winona. They have conventions all over the world. I've only been to Winona, but I'd like to go to Wisconsin when it comes there. The *Farrier's Journal* has a listing of all these conventions."

I tell him, "I had a friend who said, 'I hate to hear that sound of the back hoof hitting the back of the front hoof.'"

He replied, "That can happen for a number of reasons. Interfering back feet can hit the ankles halfway between the ankle and the knee on the inside of the front hoof because the foot isn't balanced right.

---

9 Open shoeing- Farriers set a side a day when customers can come in anytime during business hours to have their horse's hooves trimmed and shod.

There can be many things that cause sores and it can be complicated."

"How many horses do you have in your shop at a time?"

"I have two in the shop to work on most of the time, sometimes three."

"What are some of the problems you have when working with the horses? Are some breeds harder to shoe than others?"

"I've learned if a horse is nervous and starts to pull back its hoof, I just move to the next horse for a while, and then when I come back it works out better. Race track thoroughbreds can get nervous and start jerking their hoof back. It's usually after I pull the shoe, but I keep going. If a horse has an attitude and plows onto me, I push them away from me and talk rough to them and about the fourth time they stand still for me. I'm never rough with a horse. You have to earn their trust. My customers have told me three things they don't like to have their farriers do—they don't like them to be too rough or do a sloppy job, and they want them to show up on time."

This young man thought he would be back to work in full swing in two weeks; however, it was more like six to eight weeks before he could do his work and then not to his satisfaction. After his accident, he recognized his mistake. He had been tired and pushing himself over his limit.

Miller's Tin and Repair

There are many interesting different occupations in the Amish community. My finding this tin and repair shop was just by chance. I had actually come to the farm to talk with a teacher I had interviewed earlier.

As I drive up to the house, I am greeted by two dogs. Usually I am careful when there are dogs. I have been barked at and growled at, especially when no one is home. I'm very slow getting out of my car and by the time I do, the school teacher has come out of the house, and we discuss her previous interview. By the time we've finished talking, her mother and three of her sisters have stepped out of the house. Her father joins us, too, and we begin visiting.

"I have an appointment with your neighbor," I explain. "I want to find out about the Creek Ridge Sawmill. A section of my book will be about jobs and apprenticeships available for the Amish children after they finish school."

On hearing this, one daughter quietly goes into the house and comes out with a fairly large stainless steel appliance with a crank on it. Her father asks me, "Do you know what this is used for?" I shrug my shoulders and shake my head No.

"It's a stainless steel butter churn," he continues. "I had a guy who wanted the paddles remade. His churn was made of wood, but seeing the stainless steel paddles I made, he said, 'If you can make those you can make the whole butter churn."

"Do you make many things like this?"

"I work with stainless steel. My daughter has made a few things too." After making this statement, he turns and walks to his shop a short distance away. He comes back with two items—one is a stainless steel feed scoop and the other is a dust pan.

"This is wonderful," I tell him. "I'm always looking for new occupations out here in the community."

"My dad made a lot out of tin. He called his shop 'Miller's Tin and Repair'." After saying this, he talks to his daughter in their language of Pennsylvania Dutch. She goes into the house and returns with a huge covered square tin container.

His wife explains, "This is a cold-pack canner. It can hold fifteen quarts. My husband's father made this"

"What else have you made?' I ask the husband.

His wife again goes into the house and brings out a stainless steel covered cake pan to show me. He tells me, "One lady had me make a pan like this as big as her oven."

I could understand the need for a pan of that size because of large Amish families and having to serve over a hundred members on a church Sunday, (bean soup and possibly cake). A pan that large would save time when serving large numbers of people on different occasions.

One item I find to be unique is a pair of glasses. He had made a new nosepiece of stainless steel. He tells me that the glasses will be sent to a customer in Staples, Minnesota.

He then shows me a number of articles that need repair, such as handles that need soldering, plus many other items he has made. For his soldering he uses propane gas and 'Berns O Matic Map Gas' which burns hotter.

"Did you learn this trade because of your dad?" I ask him.

"Yes I did." With a laugh, he adds, "I was born a farmer. I just sold my cows. I kept a couple of the cows for our use and the leftover milk I use for the calves. I either started my retirement too soon or was too slow in retiring. "

It is exciting for me to find another occupation in the community, and fun to have the whole family sharing this interest with me.

Many Amish men change occupations in their mid-fifties, either renting out their land or turning it over to a son to farm. This is a family of five daughters and no sons to take over the farm.

Creek Ridge Sawmill

Two big German Shepherds begin barking as soon as I drive into the yard but it isn't long and they are both at my side. As I stand at the door talking to the Amish housewife, both dogs began nudging my hand. I had been here twice before, but both times her husband was gone on a business trip. I make an appointment for the following day, Saturday

When I return on Saturday, there he is, sitting on the steps reading the *Rochester Post Bulletin Weekend*. He stands and comes to meet me, telling the dogs to be quiet. After I greet him, he leads me to the open porch where there is a gray painted bench for us to sit on.

"I remember being able to buy raised glazed donuts here," I tell him. "They were the best. You used to have a shop and had small pieces of furniture to sell in the shop. Don't you have two sets of twins? How many children do you have?"

He tells me that he and his wife have ten children. The two sets of twins are boys. There are three other boys and three girls. Two of his sons work with him in the sawmill. Besides running the sawmill, he also farms twenty-eight acres.

"How did your interest in sawmills begin?"

"I worked at a sawmill as a boy and then worked three or four more years for a guy who ran a sawmill. He made the logs, sawed

Creek Ridge Sawmill.

and built pallets. I started sawing for a shop I built in 1995, I didn't start my own sawmill until 1999."

"Your sawmill has really grown since then. Are you as busy as other mills in the community?"

"Probably. I buy logs from local loggers in Decorah, Iowa, and Houston and Rushford, Minnesota. I process them and sell to pallet companies in Cresco, Tasselers Pallets in Waterloo, Iowa, and to a broker in Owatonna who in turn sells to pallet shops. I also sell railroad ties to Shalley Jones Coop in Canada. I saw for log cabins, too."

"How do people hear about you?"

"I go to Preston and use a Fax machine, to send out billings and fax companies looking for places to sell my products. I check my faxes two times a week.

"Did you have to get a loan to start your sawmill?"

"I had to get a line of credit to buy the logs. To get 30,000 feet of logs, I would've had to come up with $10,000 to $12,000, depending on the grade. I didn't have to borrow for the equipment, though; I did that on my own. "

His sawmill creates jobs for others in his community. Besides his two sons and himself, he has two family men hired fulltime and will soon be hiring two other young men. Altogether, six or seven men will be employed by the sawmill.

A Sheet Metal Shop
(Roofing and Siding)

It is the hottest day we've had this summer. As I drive through the countryside in the heat, I see a crew of approximately eight or more young Amish men and boys gathering bundles of oats and bringing these bundles into the barn to be threshed.

I am on my way to interview another teacher and also her brother, who has a metal shop. Living on this farm are grandparents, parents and a son and his family. As I approach

Sheetmetal is made into siding and roofing in this Amish shop.

56

the first home I see mattresses lying on the porch, evidence of the family trying to 'beat the heat' to get some much needed sleep on these hot nights. They have no electricity or electric fans.

A man in his late twenties comes to meet me as I leave the coolness of my air-conditioned car. I introduce myself, and explain who I am and the purpose of my visit.

"Would you mind if I looked at your metal shop?"

"No. I don't care." He leads me up the hill and into his shop, where his two children and two of his siblings are playing. His wife and cousin are helping him in the shop. They are bending sheets of metal for siding.

The huge equipment is impressive. Modern machinery has been converted from being electrically driven to being belt driven off a drive shaft and propelled by a stationary gas or diesel engine.

The roll of steel sheeting is run through the machine to make siding for sheds and barns.

"This is quite a shop!" I exclaim. "How did you become interested in this type of work?"

"I started roofing and doing carpenter work when I was fifteen. I did that until I was in my twenties. Then I built this metal shop three years ago. I was either 23 or 24."

"Did you get a loan to get your metal shop going?"

"Yes, and if I were them I wouldn't have made the loan." He says this and laughs heartily at his joke. His laughter is contagious and I laugh, too, enjoying his humor.

This is the first sheet metal shop to come into the community since the Amish moved here thirty years ago. With the diminishing availability of farmland, new occupations such as metalworking create new jobs for the community. Since he opened his metal working shop, another young man has started a crew of three that puts metal siding on buildings and roofs. They buy their materials at this sheet metal shop.

He has not yet had any apprentices; however, he does have a younger brother and a cousin helping him. "Someday someone probably will want to learn your trade," I tell him as I turn to leave.

It seems remarkable to me that he was able to get a loan at such a young age and start a business of this size as a first time venture.

This young man's father also helped him get started. Most families will help sons and daughters financially because these same children's wages have gone to help supplement their parents' income until they are 21 or married.

A Tarp and Upholstery Shop
(Also small engine repair)

I've been to this home several times while doing guided bus tours, since this is one of the homes tourists visit to purchase quilts and quilted items. This is my third stop on a cold, damp day. I drive down the driveway, past the two houses and stop in front of the newly constructed shop. When I enter the shop, I see him working on a small motor, while two of his three small children play near him in one corner. I also see large bolts of canvas and vinyl, a huge table, and rolls of strapping material such as cotton, nylon and elastic hanging on the wall. Small engines are sitting here and there as well as some completed items made of canvas.

He is expecting me since I had set up a time for this visit.

I ask, "Can I sit on this lawn mower?[10] It will be easier for me to write and more comfortable for me if I'm sitting."

He replies, "You're welcome to sit on it. I'm making a cover for it."

"You have a huge shop. The table you work on is the biggest I've ever seen. How long have you had this shop?"

CUSTOM TARPS
TRUCKS, BOATS
INDUSTRIAL, SEWING
VINYL & CANVAS
UPHOLSTERY.

"We built this in 2005."

"What did you do when you first got out of school?"

"When I first got out I milked cows and made chairs in a furniture shop. Then, when I was nineteen, I worked for a construction crew doing some stick built houses, pole sheds, and roofing. On slow days I helped my dad make canvas tarps."

"Is that when you became interested in doing this?"

---

[10] Amish use a reel type push lawn mower.

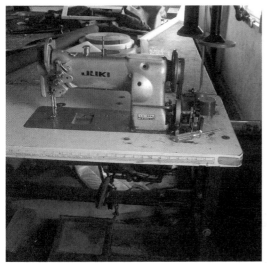
Sewing machine used in leather shop.

"Probably, but I didn't start 'til some time later. As dad's Parkinson's disease started to slow him down, I started to pick up on the tarps and upholstery."

"What did you do after you were married?"

"I rented fifty acres and farmed the land, had some cattle, and raised the calves. That was in Amherst Township. We moved here after that and I worked out of the little shop up the hill near my house. It was really cramped and I just didn't have the room to work on large items. When we built the house in 2002 I used the upstairs for my shop. I did my small engine work in the basement. My wife was glad to have me out of the house after we built this shop. Before I had the shop, I did mostly small jobs. I started sewing vinyl in the spring of 2003. I learned by doing and now I do pretty good work."

"What are some of the jobs you do?"

"Vinyl for buggies—the seats and tops—grain binder aprons, (for the Amish community), semi and grain truck covers for the English. I've gotten into a lot of different jobs."

"Who do you do the most work for, Amish or English?"

"More English lately. I've made awnings for houses, and trailers, done furniture upholstery, but not much of that yet, leather mostly."

"I suppose you're hoping to expand as time goes on?"

"Yah, that's right. I learn as I go. If I make a mistake, I start over. I had a guy come in with a Harley Davidson motorcycle who wanted the back seat on a double seated motorcycle covered. Where his wife sat, it wasn't padded and on the back of her seat he wanted a backpack made with a zipper. He wanted it to be one piece. It was difficult but I did it and it turned out real good. He was pleased with it. I also upholstered boat seats in red, white, and blue and they turned out good, too."

I could tell he enjoyed the challenge of the work he was doing and was ready to tackle whatever job came his way.

Custom-made Leather Worker
(And Farrier)

My memories of this leather goods worker and Farrier go back to a time before he started this business. He was a young single man working with a crew doing carpenter work.

His grandfather Dennis had told me grandson and wife would be moving into a house which Dennis' daughter had been using to store items for her grocery business.

The leather worker is now a family man with five children. "When my aunt gave up the house she was using to store grocery

A hoist is outside the leather and ferrier's shop for moving heavy equipment.

items," he tells me, "we built her a storage shed. Later, we built her a grocery store. Then I used the storage shed as my first shop." [11]

"What did you do those first years you were married, before you had a shop of any kind?"

"I had a fulltime job working for a dairy farmer. I eventually started sharpening reel type mowers. It was a challenge because they weren't easy to sharpen. Then, when I had my first shop, I made sleighs and wagons."

"Where did you apprentice and learn the trade of working with leather?" I ask.

"I just learned by doing," he replies. "I've been in this business sixteen years now."

"When did you start shoeing horses?"

"I shoed my first horse when I was twelve." He asks me, "You know John H. don't you?" I nod my head that I do. "I started shoeing horses when he quit. He was a farrier for the community. Do you know what a farrier is?"[12] I admit I've never heard the term. He explains, "It's a name for those who shoe horses."

11 His Aunt first had storage in the old house on the building site and her store was in the back porch of the larger home on the site.   A storage shed was built and later a large store with room for storage.
12 A Farrier – pertaining to iron, a worker with iron, a shoer of horses or a blacksmith, Webster's Encyclopedia of Dictionaries.

"Have you apprenticed anyone here in your shop?"

"I don't apprentice anybody. I usually hire help. It's mostly family or a neighbor. My son helps in the shop, too. This will probably be a family run business. The last hired man is moving on in the shoeing business and starting up on his own. I had a brother who worked here, and he went off on his own shoeing, too. I won't be doing it anymore, but I will still sell the shoeing supplies for the local farmers. Two 'English' guys worked for me but they only started out here to get a 'hands on' feel for it. They went on to school, because they wanted to work with 'show horses' and get into bigger things."

I ask, "Where are these schools?"

"There is one in Ardmore, Oklahoma, and another someplace in Minnesota. There are a lot of shoeing schools. In a one hundred mile radius we could probably find fifty or more farriers. They come here to get their supplies. Local guys come here, too."

"So you give jobs to family and neighbors?"

"I like to keep it on the smaller size and do the work myself. I don't like a lot of employees in my shop."

"What kind of leather work do you do in the shop? Do you make mainly harnesses and bridles?"

Work bench in leather shop.

"No, I'm bigger into saddles. Harnesses and bridles are a small part of the business. I'm not into retail. I have small companies I make hunting bags for, mostly the caps on the arrow holder. They want the 'old look'. I also do some trim with fringe and do other supplies made out of leather. A guy out of Winona, Minnesota, distributes to sporting good catalogs. Another is called 'German Ridge' out of Owatonna, Minnesota. I make dog harnesses by the hundreds for him. I do work for Cam Car out of Decorah, too, making caliper holsters for machinists. Another outlet in Decorah is Ozzie's Outdoors. I make bow and arrow containers called 'quivers' for them, too.

"How did all these people and companies find you?"

"I didn't go looking for them. They found me, and a lot of it is 'by word of mouth'."

I tell him, "I was told a long time ago, you didn't like to have tourists. I can certainly understand that. You wouldn't get much done."

"I used to have a couple of tour guides who stopped in," he said. "I tried to be nice. The tourists would 'ooo' and 'ahhh',' but they got in the way of my customers. One time I had about nine customers in the shop. A group of tourists come in and they crowded around me asking questions. My customers were pushed to the back of the room. One customer, who had been pushed to the back of the shop in all this commotion, spoke up, 'Was it you who put that sign up outside saying, 'No tourists'!" I said, "'Yah, I guess it was.' You should have seen the shop clear out! I thanked that customer for what he did. I haven't had much trouble since."

Many of this man's actions and ways remind me of his grandfather Dennis. Another interesting fact about him is that, as a young man, he was hired by Vernon Michel to work on the 'Old Barn Resort'. He was only twenty at the time.

Miller's Machinist Shop

On the mailbox arm is a lever from a grain binder which identifies the machinist's homestead. It is around eight in the morning. There is a heavy mist in the air and it has been raining off and on since last night. When he sees my car, he comes out of the house. He is a man of thirty-three who moved here from Ohio just ten short years ago. He and his wife have six children. I introduce myself, telling him I was here a day or two ago only to find him gone.

I ask him," Will you take me through your shop and explain what the purpose of each machine is?" He agrees, and when I enter the shop, I see it is fairly new and full of very large pieces of machinery. I also notice that every machine is belt driven off a drive shaft and propelled by a gas or diesel engine as seen in all Amish shops. He often reinvents machines for use in the Amish community and makes parts when they are required. He also does jobs for the English.

He moves to the first machine and explains, "This is a radial arm drill press, and it has up to a six inch drill bit. The arm can move in a radius of ten feet at a 360° angle. It is a 1936 machine." Moving on into the shop he points out an engine lathe explaining its use in making shafts. "We make our own buzz saws to fit a pulley as well as other machines."

"These are huge machines but they're actually very precise in making small parts?" I ask, "You must have to reinvent some parts for the equipment used in the community."

"Yes, I do. We can't really buy parts and what we need is hard to come by or it is spendy (expensive), if we can find it."

"This is a milling machine. I make key ways with this." He demonstrates for me how a milling machine works, maneuvering it to show me several cuts in a small piece of metal and then taking it over to the engine lathe to show me how the 'key way' fits precisely onto the shaft which has also been made with the same precision.

He also has a turret lathe, a Warner and Swasey production machine. "Ten years ago you could still buy this new. I was told that three guys, all in their seventies, were making five or six of these machines a year in Cleveland, Ohio."

"How much do you think it cost you to start up your shop?"

"I suppose I paid about $2,200 or $2,300 for the lathe, $1,500 for the milling machine, $1,200 for the drill press, $180 for the hack saw, and $50 for the punch press. I didn't get started right away. I worked away from home in a woodworking shop, but I kept planning for the day I'd have my own shop."

"When I was in Ohio," he went on, "a friend of mine was an English guy who was dealing on machines himself. I told him to watch for used machines for me, and if he saw a good deal go ahead and buy it for me or let me know about it. I used some of the equipment in Ohio but moved it together under one roof after I got here."

3 in one table for making rustic log furniture.

"So you really didn't get started fulltime 'til you got here. Do you think you had a talent for this at a young age?"

"Oh I don't know about that. If you have a knack for it, it will work. If you don't, it won't work."

He walked over to one more machine. "I'm making this for a guy who's going to make log furniture."

"You mean you're making this machine from scratch?"

"Yes, it has a drill press mounted to it, a tenon cutter and a chop saw. I'm making all three onto a single table. It will be one unit."

"Is it for an English guy?"

"No, an English guy would have electric. I do most of my work for Amish but I'm not limited to that."

I then ask, "Have you had others here working with you?"

"A brother helped me for a while and I had a fifteen year old put in some time."

"It must be good to get the hands-on experience. Speaking for myself, I can many times learn faster by seeing and doing rather than by reading. I know it was that way for me when I was learning how to use the computer."

"Yah, I look at it this way: you can get a college education without having to pay for it."

While we are talking, three of his children come into the shop, followed by their mother. "It's time for you to get the children to school," she says.

As we ended our conversation and I headed for my car, I can't help but ponder his last statement: "I look at it this way. You can get a college education without having to pay for it." How true this is in the Amish community.

Custom Furniture and Windows

Sam is a young man of seventeen, the oldest boy in a family of ten children. His father has eighty acres of land. Sam helps with the farm work and milking.

His grandfather made windows for the Amish community as well as for others. The grandfather became notorious when one of the more well-publicized conflicts concerning Amish belief and state law collided. It was a court case known as "The Amish in Fillmore County vs. The Slow Moving Vehicle Laws of the State of Minnesota." [13]

When Sam first began making woodcrafts and his sisters were making baskets, they worked out of a small shed. He made the frames for the baskets as well as other small woodcrafts.

The first winter after completing his eighth

This young man, at age 17, had a business with his father.

13 See the book: *The Amish of Harmony* by Drucilla Milne: Part III 'The Amish and English': Government and State Law, pages 97-100

grade education, at the age of fourteen, Sam designed bird-houses. One had a hip-roof like many barns have and the other had a pitched roof. The following spring and summer he began making these bird houses. The bird-houses were unique because of the material they were made from. It was the reed used in making baskets.

Belt driven modern machnery in furniture and window shop.

That first year Sam sold approximately four hundred and fifty bird-houses. He was surprised at how well these simply made bird-houses of reed sold!

While he was still fourteen, he went to his uncle's shop to learn to work with wood and to use the machines for making windows and furniture. These were belt driven machines which were powered by either a gas or diesel engine.

After working in his uncle's shop, he and his family used the small shed as a shop for three more years. His father decided the cramped space being used for the woodworking business, a finishing room, and basket weaving was inadequate. The year Sam turned seventeen; they began building a huge woodworking shop with a staircase going to a second level. His sisters used the upper level for basket weaving and he, at the age of seventeen, had a shop with all the equipment needed for making the furniture, windows, and bird houses.

I ask him, "What do you do when you're not in the shop?"

"I've been doing carpenter work," he replies "I like that too."

"What do you like best, working in the shop or carpenter work?" I inquire.

Without hesitating he replies, "Carpenter work, but I like doing both."

"Do you get your patterns from pictures or something you've seen?"

"I make my own patterns. I might have seen them but I make my own patterns."

I ask him, "Were you a good student in arithmetic?"

"No, but I'm good with the tape measure. I can look at the tape and know when my measurements are right."

This young man relates well to people. He is a young adult who has made the most of his talents and is enjoying his trades.

Furniture Craftsmen

There are many Amish furniture craftsmen in the Harmony/Canton area. They custom make furniture to order, as well as building kitchen cabinets for local people. One craftsman may specialize in tables and hutches, while another may build beds and dressers or chests of drawers. Many times these craftsmen make the furniture with only a picture and measurements that have been brought to them. By specializing in particular types of furniture, they help each other out, since no one worker can monopolize the business.

These craftsmen have shipped pieces all over the United States and to Canada. One older worker has shipped furniture to England, Israel, Japan and Korea. Some Amish builders hire a trucker and deliver the furniture themselves. One such man has made deliveries in all the states except Maine, New Hampshire, Alaska and Hawaii. He hopes to visit Maine and New Hampshire but probably not Alaska. Hawaii is out of the question, since the Amish do not travel on airplanes.

The advertising these artisans do relies mainly on word of mouth. Their talents and superior workmanship in this way speak for themselves. People from all walks of life and from all over the world have come into Amish furniture shops to admire the skills and talents of these craftsmen.

An Interesting Couple
An Unexpected Occupation

As I mentioned previously, I sometimes unexpectedly find the Amish involved in different occupations as I drive through the countryside. When I enter this farmyard, little do I know that I am about to come upon one of the most unusual occupations so far. After I park in front of the newly built home, I wait for someone to come onto the porch to meet me. A young woman appears on the porch and as I get out of my car, I ask, "Is your dad home?" I had talked to him briefly a few days ago but wanted more information concerning the gravestones he makes for the Amish community.

"Yes, he's in the shop. Come in and I'll go get him."

I ask, "Is your mother also here?"

"She's in her shop working on dentures."

My mind comes to a halt on the thought, 'She makes dentures?'

This is too good an opportunity to miss, so I ask, "Could I visit with her, too?"

"I'll see if she has time to come into the house."

I sit down at the harvest table to wait. The home is spacious, uncluttered, and furnished with oak furniture. There is an ironing board set up where the daughter has been ironing with an old-fashioned clip on iron.[14]

Her father is the first to enter the kitchen.

I ask him, "Does your wife make dentures?"

He replies, "Yes, she does, but she only makes the dentures—no shots or other dental work. She learned from a lady in Ohio who does this. She started because she wanted to help our community. It's very expensive to have dentures made, and she thought she could save on the cost if she made them herself."

His wife also comes in and quietly sits at the table with us. She is neatly dressed in a clean

Dental chair used by Amish woman who makes dentures.

blue dress of their Amish style and, even though she comes from a humble background, she has a quiet and professional air about her. My first question to her is how she ever got started making dentures and what kind of training she has had.

"I never thought I would be making dentures," she tells me. "It was while we were visiting in Ohio, I became interested after seeing someone there making dentures and wondered if I could learn. I decided to try it. At first it was hard for me but I continued to try."

She bought the supplies and learned by trial and error after observing the procedure on only the one occasion while visiting in Ohio. She purchases her supplies from a dental laboratory supply company.

---

14 The separate iron piece (called a 'map iron') is heated on a wood-burning stove until it is very hot and then it clips onto a tin frame with a wooden handle. Amish have no electricity in their homes or furnaces for heating homes.

At first she did all her work out of her home. When her Amish community came to have dental impressions made her clients would oftentimes have to stay and because of this wait, her family often had extra people for meals. After her business picked up, her husband suggested making an existing storage shed in back of their home into a shop for her. They remodeled the shed, adding four feet and putting in new windows for more light and good ventilation. This former shed is now the shop where she does her denture work.

Like Amish midwives who began their work for the convenience and service of their community, she too began supplying dentures.

Amish Gravestones and Burial Procedures

"Can you tell me more about the engraving you do and the stones you make?"

"My dad used to do this in Ohio. 'Old Dennis'* did it here but he said 'Your Dad used to do this and you used to help him so it's only right you take this over.' I was willing and took on the job."

"What else were you doing at the time he asked you to take on the job of making and engraving the stones?"

"I farmed."

"How many acres did you farm?"

"I farmed seventy-eight acres and worked out doing carpenter work. I just quit farming and had an auction sale. I'm going to go to grass and pasture cattle in the spring and sell in the fall. I'm in the process of setting up a shop for furniture now."

"So making the stones is a service for your community. It isn't something you can make a living at."

"No, I get paid a small amount."

His wife adds, "He makes markers for Loyal, Wisconsin and Viroqua, Wisconsin too."

"I make wooden markers until they get the real marker," he explains. "The cement stone goes in about a year later. It gives the earth time to settle before the stone goes in."

"What are the grave stones made of, cement?"

He replies, "That's right, it is mixed just like cement only we add to it."

"Yes," his wife adds again. "There is silicone sand added to the cement. It makes it smoother and tougher; I press in the letters and numbers, into the stone and put the name, age to the year and day of their death."

* see Part VIII-Other Stories: Old Dennis

"Is it true that your loved ones are embalmed but no cosmetics are done to hide the bruising or cuts in the case of accident victims? I was at one wake and every bump, bruise and cut showed."

"No, that must have been the choice of the family. Usually we allow that but we want to keep everything as natural as we can."

"I was told you use a rough box."

"Yes, we do but that is put into the ground and waits there until the pine coffin is put into it and then a lid is slid over the coffin. John makes the rough boxes and the pine coffins."

They lived in this woodworking shop while building their new home.

"Do families have the body brought back after embalming so they can dress their loved one themselves?"

"Yes, we do dress and take care of that. Then we put them on a board covered with a white sheet until after the viewing and the funeral service. The bodies aren't put into the coffins until they are ready to go to the cemetery. Everyone views and the family is the last to view before that time."

"I read someplace that you speak the words to songs at the graveside, is that so?"

"No, we sing one song. If it is a child, we sing something different.""

As we are finishing our visit, I ask if I can see his wife's and his new shops. Her shop is quite small and has much natural light and is very clean and sufficient for her work. There are impressions of teeth and dentures in many stages of repair and completion.

His shop has many windows and is also bright and full of light. He tells me, "We lived here in the shop until the house was built."

She says, "For two months while we were building the house, I didn't work in my shop. I had a lot of catching up to do when I began again. I had about fifty who were waiting for me to open up."

There has been quite a change of pace for this couple now that they are advancing in age. The farm auction and new vocations make their lives different but they are still very active and resourceful.

Custom Made Flooring

As I drive through the Amish countryside, I notice a sign, 'Custom Made Flooring'. I find a number of Amish places of business in this way; I also hear of or am told about jobs or businesses throughout the Amish community. A large truck turns into the lane, and I follow it. The truck has writing on the side advertising a business.

I pull up my car near the truck and take my time getting out of the car. In the meantime, the truck driver and the owner of the business have greeted one another and are standing near a load of old wood piled high on a flatbed wagon. As I approach these stoutly built men, I am surprised at the resemblance they have to each other, despite the fact that one is bearded,[15] and one is clean-shaven. The bearded man is dressed very plainly in hand made broadfall pants,[16] and a blue shirt, (all hand-made), while the other one is in store bought jeans, a T-shirt, and tennis shoes.

Noticing their resemblance, I ask, "Are you two brothers?"

"Why do you ask?"

I reply, "Because you look alike." They laugh. "If you'd shave off your beard, you would really look alike."

They admit they are brothers and when I ask if I can interview the young man in street clothes, he says, "I'd rather not."

In defense of his brother, the Amish man says, "There are others who have been out longer than him."

I know this is a sensitive subject and change the focus when I ask, "Can I visit with you about your shop?" He quickly agrees, and I ask, "What do you do in your shop? The sign by your driveway is down but I thought it said you do flooring."

"That's right, I do all kinds of wood flooring—oak, walnut, hickory, hard maple, butternut, and coffee-bean—anything they want."

"You must do flooring for both your Amish community and the outside communities."

"That's right, I do, and I work for others, too. I have sales in the state of New York, for a company called, 5 Star Flag Company. I sell

15 Among the Amish, a clean-shaven man is single, an Amish man having a trimmed beard only on his chin is baptized, and a man with a full beard is married.

16 Broad fall pants are homemade trousers worn by Old Order Amish men. Instead of a front zipper, the closure has a broad flap of cloth that is buttoned shut. When seen on clotheslines, the waists of these pants look very large as the pockets are stretched straight out from the waistband. When the pockets are folded into place, buttons can be seen that are used to button onto the flap, which has button holes.

to Connecticut, and around here Iowa, Wisconsin, Illinois, and Minnesota."

He then tells me that he started his shop three years ago. For ten or twelve previous years, he had other jobs. His answer to where he got his machinery brings in a local connection. "My brother and dad told me they'd heard that Root River Hardwoods in Preston had an old machine for sale so I went and bought it.

"What are some of the things you do in your shop?"

"I have red oak and white oak beams from old barns around here. One neighbor saws them into boards; another neighbor planes them and brings them back for me to straight line for flooring and molding."

""See that old red truck over there?" he asks, as he points over my shoulder. "It's a 1952 Ford. The guy wants me to put a new bed of tongue and grooved flooring in it."

"You do a lot of things here."

"Yah, I even sold an Englisher couple an old open buckboard and seat. They were getting married and they fixed it up for their reception. They painted it, recovered the old seat, and did a lot to it. When they finished, the wagon was nice. They even put it in the reception hall for their celebration."

His brother is listening as we are talking. I draw him into the conversation by saying, "I think that many who have left the Amish community got their work ethic from their roots and this contributes to their success on the outside." He agrees and visits with me some concerning this topic.

These two men are part of a family of fourteen who moved here in 1988 from Ohio.

Some Closing Thoughts

Traveling in the Amish community and meeting Amish families, I have run across many interesting people. I have found inventors and entrepreneurs—resourceful people who have recognized the needs of the community and used their ingenuity to find ways of supporting their families. They are very professional and capable in searching out new outlets for their talents and businesses.

History provides countless examples of men and women of great knowledge who contributed much but did not have a college education. Instead, they pursued their own interests and talents which led to great discoveries and accomplishments.

The Amish try very hard to remain 'least progressive,' but progress is seeping into their lifestyle. When the Amish are working for Englishers on farms, for example, modern technology is involved when they use electric milking machines (on their own farms, cows are milked by hand). In carpentry, Amish workers use electric tools that belong to English contractors, whereas in their own shops they use gas and diesel engines, not electricity. This is what I term "a temporary use". Even though they will work in 'our world' where the technology exists, these families continue to live without the material things produced by technological advances. The Amish approach to technology may be confusing to those of us who witness their seemingly double standard.

They also use our technology when it comes to medicine, travel (buses and Amtrak), and communication (telephones and fax machines.) Often, their use of our telephones, modes of travel, hospitals, clinics, doctors, and medical knowledge is for

health reasons. By not allowing modern technology in their homes and on their farms, they can still 'live in the world' without being 'of the world'.* As I mentioned before in my introduction, the Amish belief in living a simple life is based on specific Bible verses. The Old Order Amish see living in a modern world as a continually ongoing battle.

Amish bishops have expressed concern about the changes taking place because of the current exorbitant land prices. Twenty years ago land prices were affordable to them, but the land is now unattainable. This is a threat to their ideal lifestyle where their children grow up to pursue trades that allow them to remain on the farms and building sites where their parents and grandparents live. Their traditional lifestyle is increasingly coming under stress because of the shortage of land and the difficulty of accommodating large families.

* Read more in *The Amish of Harmony*, Part I, 'Getting to Know the Amish of Harmony-Living in the World but not Being of the World', Pages 19-25

Part V

Healthcare In the Amish Community

Conversations Concerning County Aid

A Wake Up Call: Polio

Amish Women: Quilting for a Cause

Caring Hands: Home Care in the Amish Community

Busy Hands and a Determined Spirit

An Unexpected Source of Help: Mary Ann McNeilus

My First Meeting With Mary Ann McNeilus

Preface from Mary Ann McNeilus' book *God's Healing Way*

Birthing and Midwives:
Secrets Concerning Childbirth
Interviews With Midwives

Healthcare in the Amish Community

The following information concerning healthcare was given to me in interviews with members of the Amish community. After transcribing the initial interviews, I took the material back to them so they could give their approval before the book's final printing.

The Old Order Amish Community puts its faith and trust in God's care. The basis of this belief lies in the Bible-Mark 12:14-17; Mt. 22:15-22; Luke 20:20-26—where Jesus teaches his followers to "Render to Caesar the things that are Caesar's, and to God the things that are God's." For this reason they choose not to carry any form of insurance—health, fire, wind or life. They feel having insurance policies would show their lack of faith in God.

Besides not believing in insurance policies, the Amish also will not file for social security coverage. By law, the Amish are required to carry special cards that exempt them from paying social security taxes. Therefore, the Amish do not benefit from the services provided by social security tax dollars. Their primary allegiance is to God, not to government.

Conversations Concerning County Aid

Over the years the Amish families have experienced catastrophes which they have quietly accepted. They trust God's hand is in all things. He uses even these tragedies for His good. I have been told about and have seen many of these personal struggles.

On one occasion while visiting Amish friends, I saw and felt the difficulties concerning the health of a husband/father who had the serious illness of Parkinson's disease. The family owned a building site but had no farm land to bring in an income. The family made and sold crafts, but this business definitely did not generate enough income to support the family and care for the invalid father.

The eldest son in the family contributed to the family income by working for a non-Amish farmer.[17] This son, however, lost his life in a farm-related accident. His death added even more stress and grief to the family's life.

Concerned about the family's struggles and grief, I expressed my thoughts to another Amish family and said, "If anyone is eligible for

---

17 Children who are under 21 and work away from home turn their wages over to parents to help support the family. When they leave or begin a craft such as woodworking, etc, the father supplements this young adult's choice of work.

county assistance, this family qualifies." The Amish knew, however, that the family wouldn't consider outside assistance as long as they could somehow manage on their own. Some weeks after I made this statement, I had a surprise visitor.

My husband was out doing the farm chores when a horse and buggy drove into our farmyard. As I watched buggy approach, I realized it was one of the bishops of the Amish community.

I invited him in, gave him a cup of coffee and put a plate of cookies on the table. He was a pleasant man, with a long white beard and dressed in plain clothing. As we sat enjoying our coffee we visited about the crops, weather and our families.

I had been wondering about the family that was dealing with such tremendous health and economic problems. I asked the Bishop if seeking county aid for health situations was allowed by the Amish community. He told me, "We prefer to take care of our own people."

I thought at the time that the statement was admirable, but such an approach seemed to me to not be very realistic, especially when unforeseen catastrophes happen. Healthcare costs also keep rising while incomes do not.

The bishop asked me if a certain Amish family was receiving county aid, to which I replied, "I wouldn't know, but you could ask the family and they would probably tell you. You wouldn't find anything out by going to the county office because the information you want is considered confidential. Why? Is it a problem if the Amish receive county aid?"

His reply was once again, "No, but as I said before, we would rather take care of our own people."

Health facilities in the area do refer families in need to county programs and other free clinics, keeping them informed of what help is available for many situations and problems. This information is also passed on to the Amish community. When necessary the Amish will seek out these programs, but as soon as the health need is fulfilled, they go off the programs. Such use is what they might term "a temporary necessity."

On another occasion several years ago, while I was visiting one of the Amish leaders, he told me of a small community hospital that sent a bill to one of the leaders stating the medical debts that had been incurred by the Amish. The letter requested that the Amish community make an effort to pay the expenses they had accumulated.

The Amish called together the people of the church districts, along with the bishops, ministers and deacons, to discuss this problem.[18] At this meeting the church members and leaders decided to have a fund drive throughout the Amish community. Along with the drive, it was also suggested that each family that was responsible for a debt begin paying whatever they could afford on a regular basis. This would establish good faith in their attempt to eradicate the debt.

The Amish often help each other in cases of need. The deacons— leaders in the community—seek out those who have a need and report their situations to the council of leaders and church members. When a suggested amount of financial aid is established, deacons go out into the Amish community and knock on doors and begin collecting these funds. I was told everyone gives according to their means, some give more and some give less. In the end, the donated amounts usually come close to the amount required. Deacons may also negotiate with healthcare facilities to reduce the acquired debts.

The Amish attitude towards insurance and social services shows how they attempt to rely strongly on their beliefs. Their independent spirit and their widespread community support system are admirable.

A Wake Up Call: Polio

Besides the issue of insurance, another aspect of modern medicine which the Amish view differently from their English neighbors is that of vaccination. The Amish do not normally believe in being immunized for diseases. This follows the same reasoning they have for not carrying any insurance policies.

The decision of whether or not to be vaccinated, however, is up to individual families. A good illustration of Amish attitudes towards vaccinations was a 2005 polio outbreak. The following is from an article in the *Fillmore County Journal* on October 24, 2005; 'Local health officials inform the Amish about polio:

Fillmore County Public Health Director, Sharon Serfling, said that the county health staff has met with Amish leaders in the area to provide information about the polio virus and to encourage the Amish to get vaccinated.

State health officials have confirmed five cases of polio have been found within an Amish community in Central Minnesota. The polio virus has shown up in the stools of the five cases, which so far have not shown any paralytic symptoms. The

---

[18] At the time of this writing there are six bishops, nine or ten ministers and four deacons.

disease first showed up in a child who was hospitalized for health problems unrelated to polio. There is no evidence of any Amish in Fillmore County having been tested positive for the virus.

Some people choose not to be immunized for religious and other reasons, including the belief that immunization may cause autism. Serfling said that there is no link between autism and immunizations.

"On Tuesday and Wednesday we met with leaders in the 13 different school districts within the Amish community," Serfling said. "We informed them about polio and urged them to get immunized."

Some people are not aware that the use of the live (polio) virus vaccine stopped in the United States in 2000 because it caused about eight cases a year of paralytic polio.* This was reflected by one Amish woman in the Harmony area who stated, "We are afraid of the vaccine. We may get polio if we take it."

While some of the Old Order Amish community near the Harmony/Canton area tended to decline the immunizations, a more progressive Amish community near Granger, MN, accepted the vaccinations. The Fillmore County Public Health Department set up immunization clinics at several of the one-room schools and a few homes in these areas.

This humorous story was related to me by a young Amish girl in her early 20s soon after the County had set up the sites where the vaccine for polio was to be given.

'A little Amish girl, age four, had been brought to the one-room school with other siblings for their vaccinations. After this little girl received her polio shot she was upset and angry. With her hands on her hips and tears in her eyes, she angrily let the county nurse know how she was feeling about the vaccination. This little one only spoke Pennsylvania Dutch.[19] Even though the county nurse did not understand the words, she certainly understood the meaning behind the girl's outburst.

The mother was embarrassed by her small daughter's display of anger. "She has behaved better at other times when she's been to see the nurse."

* www.kstp.com 5 eyewitness news
19 Children under the age of 6 normally do not speak the English language. They only speak Pennsylvania Dutch/German and only after entering the first grade are they taught the English language

Amish Women: Quilting for a Cause

Women of the Amish community are renowned for the beautiful quilts they make. These quilts are sold to the English and become a source of income for the Amish. At times, however, the quilts are a communal effort to help a family in need. The money the quilts bring in is put towards a family's incurred medical bills or help in some other financial dilemma.

One family, for example, had dwarfed twins. One of the twins had serious medical problems and was hospitalized three times over the ten months of the infant's short life. The women of the community had several quilting bees, during which they made three quilts. These quilts were then sold to help pay some of the debt incurred by the twins' family. The quilting was an effort of Christian service and support in a time of need.

I have also known of instances where quilts have been made and given to hospitals and clinics to show appreciation for the good care given by the people of the facility. It is not uncommon to see such quilts displayed in these clinics and hospitals.

CARING HANDS: Home Care in the Amish Community

When illness invades our lives, most of us would choose to live out our last days in the comfort of our homes. For the Amish it is the same; provisions are made even unto death. It is very important to be surrounded by the familiar lifestyle of their Old Order Community.

There may be some needs that cannot be filled by the family and community, but with the outside help of physicians, nurses, hospitals and county aid, good care is provided.

Busy Hands and a Determined Spirit

My friend was always busy whenever I stopped by for a visit. In the 27 years I have known her, this has always been the same. Even when she faced illnesses, she continued to show the same determination with which she approached all of the chores she had done in her lifetime.

One time while I was visiting her, she was sharing her many home remedies with me and I was copying the ones I was interested in having. A niece came in through the summer kitchen to see her aunt. On entering the main kitchen, she asked what we were doing. Her aunt replied, "We're 'busy sitters'." I laughed at her description of our activities because it was so typical of her to always be busy.

Gardening was always a pleasure to her, even when it became a hardship because of health issues. When her legs began giving her problems, she refused to give up her gardening. Her solution was to have a five-gallon bucket carried to the garden for her to sit on. Perched on her bucket, she could still do the weeding and harvesting of produce. Again the term 'a busy sitter' fits her so well.

She continued to garden and do her other work with the help of nieces and nephews. Even though the children were small, their hands and feet were a great help. "They are my legs," she told me. Her meaning was apparent. She depended on these little children. As the children grew up, she turned to the next generation.

I was told by one of her former helpers who used to be 'her legs' that as children, they did not want their play to be interrupted. They knew if Auntie saw them she would more than likely call out to them, wanting a small chore done. To make sure that she wouldn't see them, they would crawl past her window on their hands and knees. When I read this to her, she smiled and said, "I wouldn't doubt that they still might do this at times."

She put a smile on my face when I witnessed her way of getting the attention of these little ones. She tapped them gently with her cane and on one occasion I saw her hook the crook of her cane under a little one's arm and gently pull the child toward her. The children loved her and enjoyed the treats she gave them for the small chores they did.

When the weather was not fit for gardening there were always other projects to keep her hands busy. Inside her home, she moved around in a chair with castors, much like a desk chair. In this way she gave relief to her sore legs. Her work included making many kinds of homemade candy, breads and sweets. She even made a homemade drawing salve which had been handed down for many generations.

Among her other chores, she repaired old quilts. Her special chair enabled her to sit and move around the quilt frame with ease. English people from many states sent her quilts. Many of these quilts had been pieced but not finished, or she did repairs on antique quilts. One

Crafting and quilting help keep a handicapped Amish woman busy.

quilt that was brought to her had all the knots on the surface. She laughed heartily when she saw this and said, "It was no quilter who attempted to do this quilt."

At one point, my friend's family felt she needed to give up gardening because of her poor health but she was still determined to continue. She told me her doctors said she should do whatever it took to keep her active. Even though the garden work was hard for her, seeing those small plants sprout, grow and produce made her feel happy and satisfied.

During those years when she was still able to garden, relief for some of her aches and pains came through a non-Amish friend Dr. Mary Ann McNeilus. Dr. McNeilus gave her some relief through simple procedures, using natural remedies and counseling her on how to lead a healthful life.

My friend went to stay in the home of Dr. McNielus for three weeks. Being the 'busy sitter' she was, she brought her quilt frame and work with her.

Dr. McNeilus changed my friend's diet completely, omitting all sugar, dairy products and meat. She ate homemade foods prepared with whole wheat flour, olive oil and soy milk

Hot and cold applications or fomentation treatments were used to alleviate her knee and hip pain and were also placed on her side and abdomen. The treatments made her feel much better.

As the years have gone by, despite age and declining health, my

Amish friend still keeps her hands and mind busy. Heart disease and other complications plague her.

She has been bedridden for three years now, only getting up with the help of a manual lift. A sister and spouse and a nephew and wife plus their many children (great-nieces and nephews) are available to care for her. The three homes are on the same farm site. The homes are connected by a summer kitchen which provides easy access from one house to another. If the weather outside is nasty, it is not necessary to go out into the rain, snow, or wind.

Several aids have been made available for her use, helping her to be more mobile. A wheelchair and lift have been furnished by the county. Her manually operated hospital bed was one of three given to the Amish when a nearby care facility replaced their beds with electrically operated ones. A nephew made her a platform to stand on because the bed is three feet high and she is so short.

At one time, this same nephew made her a trapeze which was suspended from the ceiling. This apparatus helped her move about in bed. The trapeze had to be removed, however, because straining to maneuver her weight was not good for her heart.

The county nurse comes to see her once every two weeks. The nurse checks the catheter and oxygen and also oversees any other healthcare needs and medicines.

It is heart-breaking to hear my friend say, as she often does, "Why am I still here?"

Since the at-home care of those who are ill can be an added burden to the relatives living on the same farmstead, the community comes together in faith and service to lighten the load of these families. Many in the community volunteer to come in and help care for those who are ill. My friend, for example, has volunteers who come evenings to spend the night. She also has a niece, who runs a store near Canton, who comes to care for her aunt every two weeks on Saturday and Sunday evenings.

Even though she is very ill, her hands are still busy. She works from her bed, making projects such as beaded Christmas ornaments, key chains, and small quilted and cross-stitched items. She keeps her mind active by reading and doing word puzzles. Many friends also come to visit.

There is activity of one kind or another flowing in and out of the sick room daily. The meals are brought in either by her sister or a niece who live on the same land or they are prepared by those who come to stay the night. It is an added joy that the little children living next door are in and out of their aunt's home, visiting and keeping youth and laughter present in her life. The little children are often helpers doing small chores. Their little hands can do mighty works for an ailing aunt.

The ever-flowing visiting and care is a godsend to those who have little to look forward to. Their wants become fewer and fewer while their need for comfort becomes greater. This comfort comes in a gentle touch, the knowledge of a small change of position, a treatment of a massage, or a soft-spoken word of understanding and love. When laughter fades and there is no longer a need for words, a touch and quiet reverence for the person making their passage into God's realm is all that is needed.

An Unexpected Source of Help: Mary Ann McNeilus

Dr .Mary Ann McNeilus received her medical degree at Loma Linda University of Medicine in California in 1972. In 1973, she did her internship at Mayo Graduate School in Rochester, Minnesota and her residency at McGill University in Montreal, Canada.

As a doctor, Mary Ann McNeilus became interested in natural remedies and a healthful lifestyle. She took one year of training at Uchee Pines Institute[20], a non-profit health educational and treatment facility in Alabama. Uchee Pines approaches health through lifestyles, stressing the importance of exercise, nutrition, herbs, supplements, and faith in the Divine Healer. Dr. McNeilus' interest in herbs and supplements and natural methods of healing coincides with the Amish beliefs in the same elements.*

Because of these similar interests, Dr. McNeilus and her husband Marnelle began to look for a farm in the area where she would be available to teach and care for the Amish community as well as others interested in a healthy lifestyle. This brought them into contact with the Rosheim ladies, who had almost sold their farm to an Amish family. It would have been a perfect Amish farm because it had a windmill, and the water flow was downhill. The farm was small in acreage and had a wonderful wooded area. After thinking it over, however, the Rosheims decided they didn't want to move and cancelled the sale of the farm to the Amish.

20 Website, www.ucheepines.org
* Fillmore County Journal, www.fillmorecountyjournal.com 'Local woman serves others through alternative medicine' by Jade Wangen-Features

As the years passed and the Rosheim ladies advanced in age, they decided once again to sell their farm and placed an ad in the *Fillmore Country Journal*. Marnelle saw the ad. He and Mary Ann visited the farm and felt that this was where they wanted to relocate. In August, only a short time after the McNeilus' decision to buy the farm, the Rosheim ladies once again backed out of the sale.

What happened next, Marnelle refers to as "a miracle in the form of a Halloween blizzard."

The blizzard came on a Friday Halloween night with a vengeance. On Saturday morning, the weather was bitter cold and everything was covered with ice. The wind and ice had knocked out power lines in many areas. Roads were impassable. People were snowed in, some for as long as two weeks. The Rosheim ladies realized that being isolated and trapped on their farm in The Big Woods[21] was not good. They had second thoughts about keeping the farm and living there. On Sunday, November 2nd, the ladies called the McNeiluses and told them they had reconsidered selling their farm. This was like a miracle to Marnelle and Mary Ann, who had the feeling that maybe the farm in The Big Woods was their next mission field. As Marnelle put it, "The Lord had opened a little window" that gave the McNeiluses the opportunity to own the farm near Whalen.

My First Meeting with Mary Ann McNeilus

After I began writing about healthcare in the Amish community, I heard many Amish mention the name of Mary Ann McNeilus, always with awe and gratitude. I called the McNeilus home to set up an interview with both Marnelle and Mary Ann. We met at a mutual Amish friend's home the next afternoon, a cold day in March. The night before I met them, Marnelle had picked up Mary Ann at the Rochester Airport. She had had a speaking engagement that dealt with the bird flu and returned home late. I felt privileged to have been given the time for this interview knowing how late they had gotten home from the airport the night before. Besides her busy schedule of speaking engagements while she is in the USA, she also travels to Southeast Asia and Europe, teaching the methods of natural remedies and healthful living. As a medical volunteer in the service of the Seventh-day Adventist World Service, she has worked in Thailand, Cambodia, Sudan, Africa, and Ethiopia.

21 The Big Woods: An area of eastern Fillmore County consisting off small woodlots that were once owned and used by farmers to supply wood for building, heating and cooking. Definition found in *At Home in the Big Woods* by Nancy Overcott

Mary Ann was almost as plain as the Amish in her appearance. Her hair was tied in the back with a scarf over it. She was dressed simply in a turtleneck and jumper and had on warm leggings. Her clothing was of dark colors.

We introduced ourselves and went into a small room adjoining the kitchen to enjoy the warmth of the wood burning stove and the comfort of several chairs, including two hickory rocking chairs. Mary Ann settled herself in a rocker near the warmth of the stove.

I had many questions to ask her. As she sat in the comfortable hickory rocking chair being warmed by the woodburning stove, she became drowsy and closed her eyes. I soon found that I was asking questions, but Marnelle was answering them for her.

More than once he said, "Mary Ann, wake up. Drucie is asking you questions."

"I'm listening," she quietly responded. She would perk up for a short period of time, make a few statements, and then go back to a quiet, comfortable position, resting with her eyes closed. She had another speaking engagement that night in nearby Lanesboro and another in Rochester the following week. She was again speaking on the bird flu and how to cope with and treat symptoms using herbal and holistic medicine.

Mary Ann and Marnellle live a plain lifestyle. Although they do have modern conveniences, they do not have television. Mary Ann is unpretentious and quiet by nature. These virtues and her knowledge of holistic and herbal medicines have made it easy for her to enter into the lives and healthcare of the Amish. She has helped many in the community. I had been told that while she was in Cambodia, giving people help both medically and spiritually, the Vietnamese risked their lives by crossing the border to receive her help and to purchase her book *God's Healing Ways*. The book has been published in many languages and is in its tenth printing.

The following story is the Preface of Dr. McNeilus' book *God's Healing Way*:

Night Call

One cold January evening in Minnesota, my husband and I were settled in by our cozy wood stove when the phone rang. The call was from one of our Amish neighbors. Their six-year-old daughter had developed a skin infection, which had rapidly spread from the ankles up to the knees within the past twenty-four hours. The parents had tried a few home remedies; but as the short winter day turned into dusk, their hopes faded into despair. Would I please come to see what else could be done? Quickly I packed my medical bag with poultice materials and herbal teas. Cautiously driving over the narrow snow-covered gravel road, I headed for their old weathered farmhouse.

I found the little girl sleeping on a small cot in the middle of the dimly lit room a worn blanket covered her shoulders leaving both lower legs exposed, as even the weight of a thin sheet on the sore limbs would have been unbearable. The little legs were swollen to nearly twice their normal size. Clear fluid was seeping through the pores of the taut, reddened skin. I stood there for a moment, assessing the situation— the exhausted pain-weary child, the anxious faces of the parents, and the solemn siblings hovering around the small quiet form. I silently sent up an urgent request for heavenly wisdom to meet this challenging situation. Then we went to work!

The parents were instructed to fill two large buckets, one with hot water and the other with cold water. The infected legs and feet were to be immersed alternately in hot then cold water for a total of seven changes. This contrast bath was to be given four times during the day. A charcoal or herbal poultice was to be applied to the infected area after each water treatment. We prepared garlic and other infection-fighting herbal teas to drink throughout the day. I also prescribed plenty of pure water and a nutritious diet—free of sugar, grease and lard.

When I left the home later that night, the house seemed warmer and brighter. The family was filled with new hope and courage. When I returned the next morning, the father and mother happily reported that the pain in their daughter's infected legs had definitely diminished. The family members faithfully gave water treatments, applied poultices, prepared teas, and strictly adhered to the dietary plan. The pain, redness, and swelling gradually disappeared without a single visit to the doctor's office. This household was truly grateful for God's wonderfully simple healing ways!

Birthing and Midwives:
Secrets Concerning Childbirth

To begin with, it must be understood that in the Amish community nothing sexual is mentioned in front of children. An example of this occurred when my book *The Amish of Harmony* was in its first printing. An Amish mother, whom I knew, bought the book. Later, when I came back to visit this same mother, she showed me how she chose to keep the information about 'birthing and midwives' from her unmarried daughters.

She had rewritten the information on separate sheets of paper and hidden the paper. She had then pasted clean sheets of paper over the 'birthing and midwives' section in the book so that her unmarried daughters could not read it. She had shared the material she had copied with her married daughters only.

Keeping in mind the Amish sensitivities and beliefs, I will relate what I know about the community's birthing procedures and their midwives.

At one time in the Amish community there were four midwives. One is now in retirement due to an accident which left her an invalid. Another midwife recently moved to Missouri. A third one is currently in training and a helper at this time. She began her training because her younger siblings and their wives requested she do this for their comfort. The fourth of these Amish midwives will now be quite active due to the shortage of midwives in the community.

Midwives in the Amish community learn the birthing procedures and remedies from mothers, aunts, and grandmothers who have preceded them. They do not publicly claim to be midwives. Women of their own community send for them, knowing they will oversee and coach the birthing process, giving comfort and support.

Young children are many times unaware that soon there will be a new brother or sister. Attention is not called to this upcoming event. When the time comes for the birthing of their new sibling, children are sent away from the house, usually to a close relative. Later when they return, a surprise awaits them in the form of a new brother or sister. One mother said that after she delivered a baby boy, one of her other boys asked, "Did she (the midwife) bring my baby brother in her black bag?"

One spring day, a friend and I visited a young Amish mother with two boys. They were playing in a room close by. She called my friend and me away from her four-and six-year-old boys to the entry of the house. Closing the door behind her, she whispered, "I have a secret to tell you. We're going to have a baby." Truthfully, pregnancy was very obvious, and it was no secret! However, it was a joy to see her anticipation and excitement at the prospect of another child in the home.

A few weeks later, I stopped by again. We visited and before leaving, I quietly stepped to her calendar (one of the few things on the walls of Amish homes) and, pointing to a date on it, I said, "My daughter is here. Where are you?" She stepped to the calendar and quietly pointed to a date. That summer I had a new grandson and she had a baby girl.

Interviews with Midwives

Midwife I

I do not know what to expect as I drive up the steep narrow drive of this Amish farmstead. I had interviewed this midwife some thirteen years ago. Since that time she has had many changes in her life and is now in a wheelchair. There are two homes, a larger one and a smaller one with a wheelchair entrance. I knock on the door and a voice calls out, "Come in." As I open the door of the entryway, I see the midwife sitting in her wheelchair, cleaning the honey-combs from frames. When she asks me to excuse her mess and dirty attire, I reply, "It's good to see you working and keeping busy. I didn't know what to expect since I haven't seen you since your accident."

Her accident had happened November 15, 2001. She tells about it in this way:

"A wrecker truck had been towing a semi. I was on the Amish Byway.[22] The tow truck had come up behind me. The driver had seen me at a distance but he was distracted when he drew near me and bumped into the side of my buggy. It went into the ditch and I was thrown from the buggy."

A fourteen-year-old-girl was with her but she was not injured.

"I spent four weeks in the hospital, plus I had to return because of blood clots. I received liability insurance and had help through the county and my (Amish) community. They helped me with my home care."

She had been a midwife for many years. When I ask about the number of babies she has birthed she remarks, "I never kept track. I heard a minister once say he never kept track of how many he'd baptized. He felt that was God's doing and didn't want to take credit."

This midwife was one of the first Amish midwives with whom Doctor Mary Ann McNeilus became acquainted. The doctor had accompanied her and assisted her on many birthing calls. At one time, a midwife and friend of Doctor McNeilus came for a visit from North Carolina.

22 The Amish Byway is a blacktop shoulder on the side of Highway 52 which was put in by the State of Minnesota to provide the safe travel of buggies as well as slow-moving vehicles such as tractors, wagons, etc.

Mary Ann brought her over and introduced the two midwives to each other. They talked about their profession as midwives and shared techniques. Doctor McNeilus' friend shared a technique she used when a baby does not take in air. Her advice was, "Take cold water and sprinkle that on the baby's back and it will take in air."

When I ask this midwife what she has done when there are problems in birthing, she tells me this story about the difficult birth of twins:

"The mother-to-be was in the barn helping with the milking when she felt she had to return to the house. She knew it was time. Before the father could get to the house, one baby had already been born. "

"I was milking when an Englisher neighbor came to take me to this home. The other twin was not advancing as it should have been. After assessing the situation, we had the driver transport the mother, father and me to the hospital emergency room."

Doctors at the hospital delivered a healthy baby boy, much to the relief of the parents and midwife.

Midwife II

It is a cold winter's day when I visit midwife II. She and her husband have just returned from a nearby town where they had an appointment with a chiropractor and also did their grocery shopping. I explain my interest in the role of Amish midwives and ask if she has time to talk to me. She invites me into their home, and I follow them as they begin carrying their purchases into the house.

We enter the huge kitchen with its large oak hutches, dry sink*, and long harvest table. Six young girls begin to busily retrieve the bags of groceries and to enjoy unpacking them. There are treats and surprises within the contents and the girls are too involved to take much notice of me. There are eight girls and six boys in this family.

There is a large quilt in frame in the room just off the kitchen. The girls had been quilting until we arrived.

"Should I come back later, after the groceries are put away?" I ask.

"My girls will take care of them."

"Is there someplace for us to talk privately?"

"We can sit here at the table," the midwife tells me. The table is in one corner of the large kitchen, within hearing distance of the girls.

* A dry sink: see picture on page 125. This sink has no water source and is used as a work area for preparing food, many times washing dishes and utensils in a pan of water in this sink.

This proximity surprises me, since I know the Amish are often secretive about matters that concern birthing.

She sits on a bench next to the long harvest table and I join her, getting out my notebook to take notes. Her husband comes in with the last of the groceries and stands near us. "What are you interested in talking about?" he inquires.

Since I want to give them a sense of the type of information I would like, I tell them that I would like to read to them what I had written about birthing and midwives in my previous book, *The Amish of Harmony.*

On hearing this, the father looks at his six daughters milling around in the kitchen as they put away the groceries. He turns to me and says decisively, "We'll read it ourselves."

When he finishes reading, he hands the book to his wife so she, too, can read it. "I like the way you wrote this," he says.

"I will be just as considerate in this writing," I tell him. "I will be interviewing other Amish midwives and also the English midwives who help in your community. I also plan to write about other types of health care in Amish homes and will be visiting with Dr. Mary Ann McNeilus."

"Mary Ann has accompanied me on calls," the midwife tells me. The father soon leaves us and we continue to talk quietly, remembering the girls are near.

She tells me about some of the techniques that are used to give mothers comfort—a warm bath, a hot cup of red raspberry tea, hot packs, a gentle touch and kind words of encouragement. As she talks, I get a strong impression of what a comfort this one-on-one care must be for the mothers during the birthing process. If necessary, the midwives even stay overnight.

I discover that this midwife seems quiet by nature but also that she is a kind, confident woman who enjoys helping her clients.

Midwife III

On a beautiful but cool spring day, I turn into the driveway of a home that I had been at thirteen years before to visit with midwife III. At that time she had been diagnosed with cancer and wasn't feeling her best. She'd had surgery but when the doctors suggested chemotherapy treatments, she had instead chosen Mexico and holistic medicine and purifying treatments. She has been cancer-free since.

I knock at the smaller of the two homes and am greeted by a short, pleasant-looking woman of about sixty years of age. Her husband is sitting at the harvest table, evidently enjoying coffee and conversation with his wife. I introduce myself and explain to them that I am once again writing about their community. When I ask if they will visit with me, they invite me to sit with them. I find out they have read my first book, so they are familiar with my writing. I offer to read to them what I've collected from other midwives so far. This smiling, pleasant woman responds, "Yes, I'd like to hear it."

After reading and discussing what I have written, I ask if she will tell me her story about how she got started as a midwife at the age of forty-seven.

"It was Mary (a practicing midwife) who asked me to assist her," she begins. "I told her that I didn't think I'd be much help. She did not insist or pursue the question but, the next time I saw her, on a church Sunday[23] she asked again, 'Have you thought anymore about helping me?'"

"This time, because it was a Sunday, and no business is to be done on Sunday, I put her off again."

Mary had told her that two babies were due soon. When they were born, she did go with her.

"I had never planned on being a midwife," she explains. "My husband encouraged me to try and see if I would be interested. The first two births I assisted with were very close together. One important thing I've learned is that getting mothers to relax is a big part of our work. We have to gain a mother's trust for her to relax."

"Were your children born at home?" I ask.

"Our children were all born in the hospital because I had problems."

"You still became a midwife?"

"Birthing in the hospital helped me," she replies. "I learned things that were helpful in home births."

We exchange stories of children and their reactions having to do with babies and new siblings.

She tells me of a time when she was at the kitchen table bathing a newborn in a basin. She felt like she was being watched and turned around to find a small child standing at the foot of the stairs, staring at her with a wide-eyed look of wonder.

She turned her eyes towards the father, who was present in the room.

The father went to the youngster and said, "If you saw what you wanted, you can go back to bed now." The little fellow turned and

23 See Part VI, Faith and the Old Order Church, page 97.

trotted back up the stairs to bed without a word.

After she finishes her story, I relate the conversation I'd had with one of the deacons and his wife in the Harmony area. They had told me of a book *HOUSE CALLS and HITCHING POSTS,*[24] which is about Dr. Elton Lehman's career among the Amish in and near Mt. Eaton, Ohio. The deacon and his wife had been patients of Dr. Lehman while they were in Ohio, and he had surprised them by stopping by for a visit here in Harmony. As he was leaving, Dr. Lehman left them a copy of the book and told them that a story in Chapter 4 was about them. This is their story from the book.

Checky and Becky

'As the months passed, Dr. Lehman and Phyllis continued to deliver babies in Amish homes. Eighteen months after coming to Mount Eaton, they delivered a New Year baby in an Amish home. The delivery went well and when it was over, Phyllis cleaned the instruments and packed them back into the bag while the doctor filled out the paperwork and the parents enjoyed their new baby.

"Be as quiet as you can," Dr. Lehman whispered to his wife, gesturing at the curtain partition to the side of the room. "Dr. Eberly says birthing is a top secret in these homes. None of the children sleeping on the other side of the curtain are supposed to have a clue about the arrival of a new sibling until the doctor leaves and they see the baby lying in the cradle."

As he finished filling out the forms, the room was still except for the hissing lantern and scratching pen.

Perhaps the glow of the glass lantern shining through the curtain woke the youngsters. When the doctor glanced up, he saw a pair of tousle-haired boys blinking curious, sleepy eyes at him from around the curtain. Uh-oh, he thought, this wasn't supposed to happen.

"Ver ist sella kall?" One whispered. "What's he doing here?"

His brother studied the doctor, his papers, and black bag. Suddenly, his eyes lit up. "I know who that is! Why, it's the Watkins man!"

The doctor's and Phyllis' eyes twinkled with suppressed laughter.

"So, those Amish boys have finally figured out where babies come from!" the doctor laughed as they drove away into the night. "The Watkins man who sells spices and flavorings brings babies, too!"'

The midwife smiles when she hears this story. "As children get older, when they see a midwife and recognize her, they know what

---

24 *HOUSECALLS AND HITCHING POSTS* as told to DORCAS SHARP HOOVER; chapter 4,'Checky and Becky' page 48.

that means. This is why we send them away from the house, so the children do not know that the baby is on its way.

I tell her of one fall day when I received a phone call from a neighbor who lived close to the Amish. I was asked if I would go and pick up a midwife. I also picked up the young father's mother, who would assist at the birth. The midwife brought with her a rather large bag. I drove down a long, steep, tree-lined driveway to the home, let the two women out, and turned my car around to leave. As I drove back up the driveway, I saw the midwife and her assistant pasted up against the washhouse wall, out of sight of the front side of the house. I proceeded up the hill, looking back at the opposite side of the house, where I saw that the children were being hurried out the back door and across the field to auntie's house. That was when I realized the midwives' work was a 'secret'.

We visit for quite awhile and I suddenly realize it is 6:00 PM. I still have another stop to make in the neighborhood.

As I prepare to leave, the midwife tells me, "We'll be moving to Missouri in June. The children are building us a new home. We have several daughters there. "

"It must be nice for you to know that everything will be waiting for you when you get there, including a new home."

"Yes, it is, but we will miss our children and grandchildren here."

"I'm glad I was able to talk with you before you left. Thank you for your time and good luck in your new home."

Assistant Midwife

As I drive along the country road near the farm where this assistant midwife lives, I see the young men and boys of the Amish families loading oat bundles onto a wagon. Another wagon pulled by horses is already loaded and headed toward the barn. The young man driving the wagon waves at me as I turn onto the long curving driveway. I have known this family for many years, since they were our neighbors. Our farm was just up the road from them

Grandparents, parents and three married children all live on this one farm site. Their five homes come into view. A son and his family live in the first house, the grandparents live in the second house, and another son and his family live in the third house. Further down is a stone house where a recently married daughter and her husband are living temporarily. The parents' home is connected to this stone house. Another married daughter whose husband makes furniture also lives on land that is part of this farm but not on the same site. Near the houses is a good-sized craft shop where large quilts, small quilted items, jams, jellies and garden produce are for sale.

The woman I have come to interview is the mother of eleven children. I learned just recently that she is working as an assistant midwife. Earlier, I had made an appointment to talk with her concerning her new duties as a midwife. I am anticipating a pleasant time together.

We greet each other warmly. As we walk through the door, I notice the house seems rather quiet. Usually, her single daughters are about, as are the younger brothers and a few grandchildren. I suspect the mother did not want her single girls around during our conversation because of the secrecy the Amish keep about the birthing process.

I tell her she might like to read what I have written about the other midwives before we talk. As she begins to read, I notice how quiet the house is. It is just she and I and the sound of a ticking clock. Loaves of fresh bread, baked and packaged, sit on the table, as well as two bowls of dough covered with towels.

While she is reading, her youngest daughter comes in to ask her mother a question. As the girl leans down towards her mother, she quickly turns the pages away so her daughter cannot see the written words.

Although it is hot, a little over 80* Fahrenheit, there is a welcome breeze coming in the windows. She pauses in her reading to look up and apologize for the heat in the kitchen. "I have a slow fire going because I have grape nuts (a type of breakfast cereal), in the oven. I did most of my baking early this morning while it was cooler."

There is a knock on the door. It is someone who has come to buy fresh vegetables. The midwife goes out and I reread my notes while I wait for her to return. While she is gone, her older daughter comes into the house carrying a suitcase. She is accompanied by her brother-in-law. She sets her suitcase down and proceeds to take off her bonnet.

"Have you just gotten back from a trip?" I ask. Her brother-in-law is the one who answers me.

"I just brought her back from our place. She's been there four weeks helping my wife. We just had a baby girl."

When the midwife comes back into the house, I congratulate her on her new granddaughter.

"Four weeks ago our daughter had a girl and last night our boy had a son."

"Did you assist with both babies?" I ask. Since four of her married children live on this two hundred acre farm, she has easy access to their homes during crucial times.

Instead of directly answering my question, she says, "Babies know no time. This one was born about seven o'clock in the morning."

"I heard you usually assist the midwife. How many birthings have you assisted with?"

"I've helped birth grandchildren and a few others."

"Did you have your children with a midwife?"

"No, when we first came from Ohio to Minnesota we didn't have midwives. I had my first two children in the Spring Valley hospital. Our neighbor Sara took me."

Her youngest daughter again comes into the kitchen and walks through to the back room during our conversation. We stop talking until she is out of the room. Since the home is beginning to get busy with activity, I thank the assistant midwife for setting aside the time to talk with me and take my leave.

To read more on the secrets concerning courtship, weddings, birthing and midwives see *The Amish of Harmony* page 67-74.

Part VI

Faith and the Old Order Church

Casting Lots: The Selection of Amish Leaders

Interviews With Bishops: Families and Change

The Practice of Shunning

Faith and the Old Order Church

There are six church districts in the Harmony/ Canton area. Each two church districts have a bishop and a deacon. At the time of this writing there are five bishops, four deacons and ten ministers, although usually there are two ministers for each church district. Bishops, ministers and deacons are called to their vocation by the Holy Spirit or by divine appointment (Acts: 24:2-26). Their appointment is ratified by the church and acknowledged by laying on of hands by elders (Acts: 6:6), an ancient practice of ordination.

German Bible used by the Amish.

The bishops' functions include leadership, preaching God's word, and preserving God's people from error, by watching over and caring for the religious community. In order to be a bishop, a man must have been a minister, which puts him in a mature age bracket. Ministers are the bishops' helpers and perform all the same duties—preaching, reading Bible scripture, giving communion, and performing weddings, funerals, and other church services. The deacons' functions include Bible reading, caring for the poor and taking care of temporal affairs.

Church is held in homes every second Sunday and families take turns rotating this event from home to home. The opposite Sunday is called a visiting Sunday. Collapsible benches (called church benches) are brought to the home where services will be held. There are approximately thirty families in each church district. Bean soup is served for the noon meal.

Collapsible church benches taken from home to home for Church Sundays.

The Selection of Church Leaders

Leaders are chosen by casting lots. When a church district needs a bishop, minister or deacon, the congregation gathers at one particular home. Different methods may be used for casting lots, but all baptized members of the church group give their input as to who is a man of good faith and a good family man. One method that can be used is to have every baptized member go to an open door or window where there is a person on the other side. Each member quietly says the name of a man they think has the required qualities. The person to whom they have spoken then writes down the name. It makes no difference how many times a name is mentioned—the name is only written one time. In the case of one bishop I interviewed, there were seven names spoken. Each name is then placed in a book; the books are all set on a table. One person goes to the table and chooses a book. The person whose name is in that particular book is considered to be chosen by the hand of God and cannot refuse leadership. (Proverbs 16:33: "The lot is cast into the lap, but the decision is wholly from the Lord.") Whoever is chosen is therefore believed to be led by the spirit of God to be a leader in his religious community.

Bishops are appointed for life and receive no pay. Of the five bishops in the Harmony/Canton area, two have moved—one has moved to Missouri, and the other has moved to Wisconsin. Both of these men, however, will remain bishops over the districts here in Minnesota, even though they have moved, until replacements can be made. They return for district meetings, weddings, funerals, and other special church events. They travel by Amtrak or bus because of the distance involved.

The oldest of these five bishops is ill. Despite the fact that he has been relieved of many of the duties involving this position, he is still a bishop. (Jake passed away in July of 2007 after serving 22 years and was the first bishop of this community. He and his wife, Lydia, have thirteen children.)

Bishop Interviews: Families and Change
Rather than farming or doing other work within their Amish community, Amish offspring often work outside their community. This change presents many challenges to the Old Order Amish. Farming was at one time the primary occupation. It remains an option but land is no longer available in small acres because corporate farming is taking over. Work 'outside' is frequently an economic necessity. More and more Amish now work at a trade. There are, for example, two Amish crews in Harmony who have been hired by contractors to build two new homes for English families.

Money is needed to support families who continue to grow in size. The average family has approximately seven children, with some families having anywhere from eight to sixteen children. After young people are out of school, at the age of fourteen, they work to help support these large families and also help parents pay off debts. I have witnessed families who have struggled at making a living when their children are young. Then after finishing eighth grade these same children begin to work and bring home a paycheck, which goes to parents and the extended family. The money these young workers contribute makes it easier to support the family. When they reach the age of twenty-one, these same sons and daughters can keep their wages and save towards starting a trade or buying a home of their own. By this time they have apprenticed and learned a trade. Parents often contribute to the young adult's future by helping them with the collateral they need to start their independent lives.

One bishop I interviewed has operated a sawmill for approximately twenty years. He has been a bishop since the fall of 1997. I asked him, "What are the Amish leaders' views on working 'outside' in our community and other English communities?"

"We would rather be self-employed in our own community," He replied. "Thirty, forty, and fifty years ago we could afford to farm, but now who can afford to pay the prices they're asking for land? Work also gets so far out now. We have to travel miles to get work. It is fast changing times. When we farmed, we could take off for the day, but with the sawmill we have to be here five days a week. We have to take care of business and if we are gone we hire help."

A younger bishop who is the father of seven sons (no daughters) said, "It is important to us to keep our boys at home so we can guide them. Too much separation when they are young is not good." He will soon be moving his family to Viroqua, Wisconsin, partly because he feels it is important to have farmland for his boys.

As we talked, I told him that when I had written my first book, approximately 75% of the Amish farmed. I wondered how that percentage has now changed.

"There was a time," he reflected, "when a couple had eighty acres, ten cows, six horses and machinery to farm, but now with interest rates the way they are, it's hard to borrow money. Now we have barns with no cows. I wonder if it is more like 75% these days that are working at trades rather than 75% farming."

A third bishop that I interviewed has a family of fourteen. He was a minister thirteen years and has now been a bishop for ten years. He farms 80 acres and also has a woodworking shop.

"What do you believe holds your families together during these times of such great change?" I asked. "Why do you think there are so few that leave your community?"

"What keeps the family together is our working together and the love we share."

I believe he is right. As I wrote in my previous book *The Amish of Harmony*, "Fifty and sixty years ago, when horse farming was a way of life, people had large families. Large families provided joy and helped lighten the work. Families were also more social; visiting, humor, the art of communication were the entertainment of all people. Love, sharing, caring, support, comfort, and nurturing in large families brought life into full circle. It was a wholesome country life with families getting together without all the entrapments of worldly things, enjoying the seasons of nature and family life *."

The Practice of Shunning*

I also asked the bishops other questions concerning shunning practices. A little history here will put this into prospective. The purpose behind *meidung* or shunning is to call back into the fold those who have 'fallen away' from the fellowship of the Amish life. Briefly, the Amish were originally part of the Mennonites, a group which broke away from a radical group of Anabaptists (believing in adult baptism) during the Protestant Reformation in 1525 in Zurich, Switzerland. The founder of the Mennonites was Menno Simons, a Catholic priest from Holland. The Amish are sometimes called Amish-Mennonites because they were originally part of the Mennonites but broke away in 1693. Their founder, Jacob Amman, was a Swiss Mennonite Bishop. These groups were severely persecuted for their beliefs, and in the 18th century, to escape this persecution, the Amish began immigrating to America. The Mennonites began immigrating to America in the 17th Century.

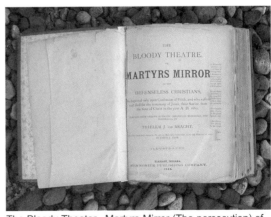

The Bloody Theater, Martyrs Mirror (The persecution) of defenseless Christians

* Read more on shunning practices in Part VII, Leaving the Amish Community, Views on Shunning, Pages 114-116

I asked all three bishops their thoughts on the subject of shunning. I wanted to know if the shunning is different for those who aren't baptized, compared to those who have been baptized and have made a commitment to the Amish way.

"Yes, it is different," I was told. "We don't shun those who aren't baptized, only those who have been baptized. They have made a commitment to God by accepting baptism. Shunning reminds them of the importance of their commitment and of the vow they've made to God. People don't understand that about us but it has always been this way. It is a part of disciplining when the church ordinance isn't obeyed."

When I talked to another of the bishops about those who leave the Amish community, he made this comment, "You didn't grow up like this. It doesn't mean you (English) can't be saved. All we have ever known is this way. It wouldn't be right for me to criticize you and your way because it would fall back on me. You have your ways of doing things and we have ours."

I believe he was telling me that each of us are brought up in a certain way and worship God in the way we were taught. For this reason, our perception of God and how we worship our Creator is right in our own minds. To judge one another is not our place— judgment is not for humankind; it is between God and the individual, not God and mankind. This bishop did not want to be judged for making a decision about me or the way I live.

Part VII

Leaving the Amish Community

Hardships Faced

Personal Stories

More Concerning Shunning Practices

Leaving the Amish Community

When a young adult decides to leave the Amish community, the situation is difficult for parents and siblings. It is a time neither cares to talk about. My intent is not to dwell on the reasons why the ex-Amish decided to leave their community but to relate what has happened to them since they left.

I have witnessed several success stories of those who decided to leave their Amish lifestyle. These young people are successful for a number of reasons. Those reasons include good work ethics; Amish families work well together and parents teach their children at a young age to be responsible and respectful. They have also learned to use their ingenuity to create jobs both in their Amish world and in the outside world.

Amish lives are family-centered both in terms of their immediate family and in their broader church-family. Outsiders question why more young Amish men and women have not left the Amish-way. The numbers that leave remain very small. I attribute this to close-knit families. All social events and work related events such as butchering, corn picking, oat threshing, barn raisings, singings, attending church services in homes—everything revolves around family.

Hardships Faced

It is interesting that most of these young adults walk away from their previous lives without looking back with regret. Even though they face many obstacles these ex-Amish seem to overcome them one step at a time. They leave without money, living quarters, a means of travel—car, truck or horse and buggy—into another type of environment, away from family and all that has been familiar to them in the past. Those who have worked with the English in the outside world, however, may find it easier to leave. Many in the Amish community work in both worlds.

To think that they will not have contact with family members is a mistake. Their roots are still very important to them and there is still that bond which will always be present. Each family has a choice as to how and if this bond will continue.

Personal Stories

A Marriage: A Former Amish Man & an English Girl

At eighteen, Dan made his decision to walk away from his Amish family. Before he left, he wrote a note to his mother. He left his mother and two sisters, determined to make it on his own. He had no means of travel—no horse or buggy—no money in his pocket and no place to live, but he did have a job working for an English farmer. The farmer and his wife gave him room and board for eight months until he could support himself. Getting a driver's license and a truck for work was his next challenge. He bought a Toyota truck and soon found himself an apartment. He took each step with determination towards his goal of succeeding.

Winters, he worked for farmers and when the weather changed he worked on his own—shingling, insulating, and siding homes in the area—doing whatever the job required. Soon, he was thriving.

He began going to sports events at the local high school. At one of the basketball games, he noticed one of the cheerleaders. Jessica was sixteen-years-old at the time. Dan knew her father owned the lumberyard in town but other than that he did not think anymore of it.

While Jessica dated during her high school years, Dan also dated, both ex-Amish girls and English girls.

The summer following her high school graduation, Jessica began working at the local grocery store, but she didn't like being cooped up inside and wanted more activity. Her father offered her work in his lumberyard on weekends and holidays. He soon found that he needed her for deliveries, so he put her in a truck and had her use the lumberyard as her driving and training field. The truck had a straight-stick shifting lever and before long she had mastered both the stick-shift and driving the truck. The real problem for her was when she had to stop on a hill and keep the truck from rolling backwards, but this too she soon mastered.

While she was working at the lumberyard, Dan would come in for shingles and other supplies. As she waited on him, they would talk. Jessica's bubbly personality and friendliness attracted him to her from the beginning.

One day she was sent out to deliver shingles to a site where he was working. As she drove up, he recognized her. He helped her unload the truck and after they had finished, he asked her if she would give him a ride into town so he could get his old Dodge truck. He used it to haul shingles and other equipment so he wouldn't scratch the pickup bed of his newer truck. He had driven his Toyota out to the job.

Dan was impressed that Jessica knew how to drive a stick-shift truck and told her so.

For two years after that, they went their separate ways. She enrolled in college to get her teaching degree, while he continued to work in the area. After graduating from college, she began teaching social studies as a part-time teacher in nearby Mabel, Minnesota.

One particular morning in February of 2004, Jessica was driving to her teaching job; at the same time, Dan was headed out of town to pick up furniture in Ohio for R & J Wood Goods of Harmony.

As she was about to turn east onto Highway 52, she noticed that he had pulled up behind her at the stop sign. She remembers how hard her heart was pounding when she saw he was following her. When she turned off at Mabel, they waved at one another and each of them continued with their day.

That evening when the phone rang, Jessica had an idea that it might be Dan calling her—and it was. He was calling from Ohio to ask her for a date. A day later he called her again—this time to tell her his truck had broken down. He was stuck in Ohio until the truck could be repaired. He finally was able to return home one-and-a-half weeks later.

Fate kept them apart again. When he reached home after spending the time in Ohio, he went to her parents' home and they told him she was in Rochester taking a graduate class in education. She was gone for the weekend, staying in Rochester with her sister.

By the time Jessica returned from Rochester, Dan had gone on another run to Ohio.

During this time, they talked on the phone, but three more weeks passed before they actually had their first date. They dated twice that same week and then began keeping steady company.

In May of 2005 they became engaged. Jessica was very busy teaching and with teaching-related activities that year. In April she was one of the Family Career and Community Leaders of America. She was in Minneapolis at a conference on a Thursday, Friday, Saturday and Sunday.

While Jessica was attending this event, Dan went home to northern Minnesota where his mother lived. The purpose of his visit was to tell her about the girl he intended to marry.

He knew it would be hard for his mother to accept his marrying an English girl. He was not surprised when his mother told him, "If you marry her, you will never be able to come home again." His response was, 'I think that is up to you, Mom, and no one else.' He left knowing that he would come home again, and he had every intention of bringing Jessica with him.

One-and-a-half years after their first date, they were married. Jessica says 2004 was a big year for her— she got her dog Mesa, a large golden retriever, she started teaching full-time, and she and her future husband began dating. In December of 2006, Jessica met Dan's mother, as well as his two sisters.

A Business Begins With Amish Brothers

Reuben and Jake are brothers who come from an Amish family with thirteen children. Jake, the older of these two brothers, began teaching at Scotland School when he was fifteen and he taught there for three years. When he was nineteen, Jake left the Amish community. At the time, he was working for a farmer in the area.

Two weeks after Jake left, his eighteen-year-old brother Reuben and an Amish friend also left. Reuben and his friend slept in an abandoned car for two nights. Neither of the boys had money to pay for food or a place to sleep, so it was necessary to find work as soon as possible. They decided their best chance of finding work would be with area farmers. Their next move was to go to the local tavern. There, they found farmers who needed help and they were soon employed working on farms.

Reuben's friend eventually went back to the Amish community. Reuben, however, was determined to succeed. His fortitude kept him striving for a better life. He worked hard and earned the trust of his employers. Before long, he had secured his driver's license and a truck of his own.

He rented several places before eventually buying a trailer house. Reuben was always looking for a way to better himself. He studied and earned his General Equivalency Diploma. He worked for Harmony Enterprises Corporation (HECO), a local manufacturing firm, and in 1985 and 1986 he went to Dakota County Technical School in Rosemount, Minnesota. He worked part-time for Anoka Electric and soon applied for a job with Dairyland Power Company of La Crosse, Wisconsin. He has now worked there for almost twenty years.

Reuben and Jake's father, an Amish bishop, convinced Jake to return home nine weeks after he had left the community. After he went back, he did farm work and carpentry work. He also began helping his younger brothers make furniture in their furniture shop. Thinking he was home to stay, Jake was baptized into the Amish religion and community.

Four years after returning to the Amish and being baptized, Jake once more began to feel restless and dissatisfied. This time when he left at the age of 23, Jake had a checking account as well as a savings account.

When I interviewed him in 2007, Jake had been out of the Amish community for eighteen years. I asked him, "Why did you leave a second time?" His reply was simply, "It just wasn't for me."

Jake walked away from one lifestyle and into another. At first he stayed at his brother Reuben's trailer. Next, he found work for a short time at HECO. After leaving HECO, he worked at Rush Products in Rushford, Minnesota, and later at Cam Car in Decorah, Iowa.

Reuben continued working for Dairyland Power Company, making good money along with benefits.

Despite having full-time jobs, Reuben and Jake found they had free time on their hands. They decided to put this free time to good use. For three years, they rented land, bought 24 to 30 calves a year and fattened the calves for market. Jake also went into partnership with an Englisher couple who had bought the historic old Selvig home, which he helped to remodel as a Bed and Breakfast. Jake and the Englisher couple later sold the business for a profit.

In 1992 the brothers committed to a bold venture. They bought a building that had been a veterinary office and turned it into a furniture craft shop; however, when liability insurance and operating costs became too expensive, they decided that the business wouldn't be profitable enough to continue. They closed the shop and made it into a business office which sold furniture and smaller items. As time went

on, a house near their shop came up for sale. Reuben bought the house and two years later the brothers bought more land that connected to the buildings they already owned. They now had 1.8 acres. In 1999 the brothers put up a large two-story storage building with a basement to display and store furniture. Reuben and Jake contract the furniture in Ohio and have it trucked to their store. Orders are made every three weeks and it takes ten weeks to fill the orders.

On the property called R and J Wood Goods is an office where smaller household items are for sale, a two-story building for storage, and two homes. Reuben and Jake are planning to add onto the larger building for more storage.

Reuben and Jake overcame many obstacles and have succeeded in making a good life for themselves.

No Regrets

When I finally tracked Harvey down—I had to reach him by cell phone—he was in Wyoming. I told him who I was and my purpose for calling. I could tell by his reaction that he didn't recognize my name until I said, "I wrote the book *The Amish of Harmony*." In a surprised voice he responded, "I remember you from when I was a little boy!" (He is now twenty-eight.) I could sense his smile as he said this.

When I replied, "Yes, and I remember you as a little boy!" As I answered him, I saw him as the little boy he once was. These memories gave us a good base for our conversation. We continued talking and I then requested an interview for my upcoming book.

He asked, 'When do you want to do that?"-

"Now," I replied. He began laughing and said, "This is not a good time." Unbeknownst to me, he was in a restaurant with his buddies, a crew of ten who work for the company which employs him. "It wouldn't work now but I have your number and I can call you later. Will that be okay?" It was 7:30 in the evening, Wyoming time. "That will be fine, "I told him. "I'll be waiting for your call."

He called me the next morning with his story.

He is from a family of four brothers and two sisters.

On the night that he left the Amish, he lay awake, waiting until the house became quiet. At two o'clock in the morning he got up and left the house. It was twenty below zero and he had only the clothes on his back. He said he'd been thinking about leaving since he was sixteen. Now, at seventeen, he had made the decision to leave his Amish community.

He knew a friend who had an apartment in town and headed to his place. In the bitter cold, he began running, wanting to reach town as soon as possible. He would run and then walk in intervals, determined to make it the five miles to town. "If I had been smarter, I would have planned how I would leave. I was almost frozen when I got to Harmony!"

That same morning his friend found work for him milking cows.

I asked, "Weren't you too tired to work after being up all night?"

"No," he replied. "I was going on adrenalin and I needed the work."

"The farmer gave me clothes to wear," he added, "but wouldn't let me get a haircut because he thought I'd go back home. After two weeks I got my first haircut. I lived upstairs in their home for two months while I worked there milking cows. When he sold his cows, I found another job milking cows. I stayed at the second farm milking cows until I got my driver's license and bought a car. I went home to visit my parents after I'd been gone two months."

"What make of car did you buy?"

"It was a 1980 Buick Regal." He began laughing and said, "It was blue with lightning stripes on it. I was a kid and thought it was cool at the time."

After buying the Buick, he could drive to work and began working for Root River Hardwoods in Preston, Minnesota. On Saturdays for one winter he helped a contractor on a house being built in Harmony.

"Did you go back to school and get your GED?"

"No, but I did join the Harmony Fire Department and got my Fire Fighter One Certificate. I also went to a couple of classes that were held in the area sponsored through Riverland Technical College in Austin, Minnesota. I am still a member of the fire department. I'm here for about 95% of the calls."

"When I met my wife my parents didn't feel good about that because she wasn't Amish. Up until that time I think they still had a little hope that I might return. We'd like to have a better relationship with them, but it hasn't happened yet. "

"How did you meet your wife?"

"I was with other friends when I first met Amy. I didn't pay much attention to her then. It was later when I was riding my snowmobile and stopped at the Kwik Trip that I saw her again. She was home for the weekend from working in Minneapolis. I saw her car and I just went over— taking off my helmet— and started talking. I already knew her mom, Carole, from the bank in Canton. My wife told me later, 'I went home and told mom—I think I met the man I'm going to marry.' "

"It was soon after that visit at the Kwik Trip that we started dating. We're married now and have two children, a three-year-old girl, Addison and Atlee, a four-month-old boy."

"I told my parents that we're now members of the Lutheran church and I've been baptized. The only thing that's different about me and the Amish is that we wear different clothes. We visit with my brothers and sisters and have a good relationship. Our girl and their children play together, even though they don't understand each other's language."

I asked, "What did Amy's parents think when you started dating her?"

"Her dad wasn't real happy at first when we started seeing each other but he gave me a chance."

Amy, however, told me that her Dad actually said, "You better not be bringing home an Amish boyfriend!"

When I asked what the best thing has been that has happened to him since leaving the Amish community, he replied, "It's having my wife and children. I've been out eleven years now. I wouldn't have had the opportunities that I've had if I'd stayed Amish."

He went on to say, "The guys I worked with at Root River Hardwoods were a support to me. Now I work for Minnowa.* I drive a semi-tractor and move equipment to locations and I'm with a crew of ten. They are a great bunch of guys. We are together a lot. One of the guys gave us the nickname "The Herd." It stuck and now we've all got t-shirts with the name "The Herd." We all stick together—work and eat together. When a few of the younger guys stay out late we say, 'Someone must have left the gate open. Part of the herd got out last night!' "

Harvey and his family live on ten acres of land. He and his father-in-law contract a few hogs and about fifteen head of steers a year.

Before we ended our interview, Harvey said, "I still have a lot of respect for the Amish and my parents." He misses his Amish family; however, he has embraced his new life. He is happy and has no regrets.

The Mason

Roman is the third child born to an Amish family of eleven children—six boys and five girls. He was born in 1969 in Canada. When he was fifteen, he moved with his family to the Lanesboro area.

---

* Minnowa Construction Inc. of Harmony, Minnesota, is a contracting firm that builds bridges.

After living in Minnesota for one year, he found a job working for an English farmer. The couple's children were gone from home and they hired Roman to be their farmhand, doing chores and field work and whatever else was asked of him.

Roman's father was a minister for three years and later became a bishop in the Amish community. When Roman was eighteen years of age and still living at home, his parents encouraged him to be baptized, which he did. Two weeks after his baptism, he left home for good. He never told his family he was leaving—he just left. He moved into the home of Sylvan and Charlotte, the English couple who had hired him as their farmhand. The couple trusted him and welcomed him into their home.

Sylvan and Charlotte were good to him. Charlotte helped Roman to get a social security number and a driver's license. After he had been working for them for some time, Charlotte found a job for him at the care center where she was employed. He enjoyed working at the care center, but he soon realized the work was not the kind that he wanted to do forever. He liked to be outdoors, and he knew he would be more satisfied with a job that allowed him to work outside. At the age of twenty, Roman left Sylvan and Charlotte's and struck out on his own.

Eventually he found a job working as a mason for a company in Waukon, Iowa. Rusty Berger owned the company; Rusty's policy, which all his workers knew, was, "You do the job right or you tear it down and start over and pay for it from your own pocket." He did not believe in paying out money for having the same work done twice. One of Rusty's employees was an older man named Delvin, who was semi-retired. Delvin acted as Roman's mentor and taught him the trade of masonry. According to Roman, "Delvin taught me well. He told me, 'If I had known you ten years ago, I would've sold you my masonry business.'" Roman worked for Rusty in Waukon for fourteen years.

When I interviewed Roman, he told me, "I came to Harmony and started my own masonry business six years ago. I remember my first job laying brick was the same day that 9/11 happened." Like most of us in this country, that day is emblazoned on his heart. He has become a good family man, supporting his family by working in the masonry business he began six years ago. He does both brick and stonework, which he claims is easier than laying bricks. "I like to do brick work best. It's satisfying to me to stand back and look at a completed job. I like the looks of brick better than stone." He attributes his good work ethic to his father who is "very particular and believes in doing a job right."

Roman does not advertise his masonry business and believes the best advertisement is 'word of mouth'. He said, "If you have to advertise and don't have enough work—it could mean you don't do good work. If you're doing good work, the job will find you."

The home he is presently working on in Rochester, Minnesota, is a house requiring 20,000 bricks.

The Deciding Factor: A Child's Health

For as long as we lived next to the Amish, they were always good neighbors. We, too, tried to be good neighbors to them. The road ran both ways—they helped us whenever we needed help to complete a job, and we helped them in whatever way we could, like neighbors often do.

One particular evening, Dan, one of our Amish neighbors, came to our farm about 6:00 PM, asking if we could take them to the St. Mary's Emergency Room in Rochester. Their four-year-old daughter Mary was very sick. The night proved to be a long one for Dan and his wife. We sat with them in the emergency room family area, while their little girl underwent medical tests. The test results showed that Mary had leukemia. We were all sickened by this terrible news. Mary's parents decided to stay in Rochester with their daughter. They asked us to stop at Mary's grandparents' farm on our way home to tell them about Mary's diagnosis. Dan told me to knock on the bedroom window of his parents' home. They would be expecting us. It was after one o'clock in the morning when we got to their farm to give them the bad news.

A few days later I paid a visit to the family to see how Mary was doing. The little girl was lying on a daybed in a large room adjoining the kitchen. She was listless and pale but somewhat better. The other children mingled about quietly while I talked to Dan and his wife. As I was about to leave, Verna, who was only a few years older than Mary, quietly handed me a small paper box she had made. I smiled and thanked her while I began opening the paper box. Inside were small paper hearts Verna had drawn with a pencil.

I was overwhelmed and pleased with this little girl's simple gesture and gift. I felt like she had given me a box full of love.

I wanted to do something to help Mary's family, so I packed a box of baked goods I had made and took them over to their house. On hearing that we'd brought food to Mary's, our Amish neighbors were more generous than we were. Three of the relatives—an aunt, parents, and a sister—gave us baked goods, jams, jellies, homemade noodles, bread and candy. We received much more than we had given.

For Mary's parents, the ensuing days were full of decisions and trips to Rochester. Since the Amish do not own or drive cars, Dan and his family made the necessary frequent long trips to Rochester by bus. The Harmony Cancer Support Group became aware of their plight and initiated a helping hand; soon other local groups also became involved. People in Harmony's small community willingly assisted Dan's family by driving, telephoning, and conveying messages to other Amish families.

While in Rochester for Mary's treatments, Dan and his wife met many people, including Mennonites, who became their friends and gave them help and support. Dan and his wife soon realized that Mary would need long-term treatments. Knowing the limitations imposed by their Old Order community, they decided to leave the Amish and become Mennonites, joining a Mennonite group who lived near Lime Springs, Iowa. This group of Mennonites used motorized vehicles and electricity. The Amish have a historic connection with the Mennonites and are often called Amish-Mennonites, so the family felt comfortable with their choice.

The way Dan explained it to me was, '"We had already made our decision to leave and told our extended families of our choice. They were not happy. Our children were still attending the one-room school nearby where my sister taught. I wrote a letter thanking my sister. The reason for the letter was that we knew our children—her nieces and nephews—were being teased by the other scholars because they knew we were leaving. My sister called a halt to the teasing. She called the scholars together in the classroom and told them to be kind to the children. It was not their fault that their parents had made this decision."

After moving to Lime Springs Dan became a furniture craftsman, then an auctioneer. Their family grew to three boys and six girls. In Lime Springs, Mary's health flourished and her leukemia went into remission. She lived to be eleven-years-old. Ultimately, a brain tumor and not the leukemia took her life.

Views on Shunning*

Jacob Amman, a Swiss Mennonite bishop who broke away from a radical group of Anabaptists during the Protestant Reformation in 1693, instituted the practice of shunning. He felt there should be a way of calling back into the church those who had fallen away from the fellowship of believers. The shunning practices of the Old Order Amish

112

define the major differences between Old Order Amish and Mennonites. Mennonites do not use these shunning practices.

Amman's basis for shunning can be found in the Bible in Corinthians 5:11: ". . .but rather I wrote to you not to associate with anyone who bears the name of brother if he is guilty of immorality or greed, or is an idolater, reviler, drunkard, or robber—not even to eat with such a one." The Amish believe that the Bible calls them to a life of separation and self-denial. Life outside of their Amish community is threatening because it could draw them away from God. Shunning is a way of reminding those who have left that they have not kept their commitment to God. That is why it is much more serious to have been baptized and then leave than to not have been baptized and leave. Those who leave the Amish lifestyle might feel hurt by their family's rejection of them. On the other hand, parents might also feel very hurt when all they have taught and believe in is rejected by their offspring.

In Amish homes family members who have not been baptized may come home in English-type clothing and yet on other occasions come home dressed in Amish clothing. I have been told that these persons are confused or this may be their way of showing respect. They are not ready to make a decision to become English or Amish. Families are supportive during this time.

At other times the shunning can be very definitive. At funerals, for example, the ex-Amish who have converted to modern living may come home to pay their respects to a loved one who has passed away; however, they may have to sit separate from the gathering of Amish.

Another approach is that the family may decide to include those who have left the community. A family elder might then request that those who have left wear Amish clothing to the funeral and be a part of the grieving family. A compromise like this would show love and respect not only for the loved one who has died but also for those who have fallen away and are also grieving.

In one case, a mother requested her ex-Amish sons come to their father's funeral and sit with the rest of the family. Her only request was that they dress in Amish clothing. Since they had been out for a number of years, clothing was provided for them. The day of the funeral, all of the siblings walked in according to their ages, including the ex-Amish sons.

* See also Part VI: Faith and the Old Order Church, The Practice of Shunning, Pages 100-101

When it comes to shunning, it is a matter of personal choice as to how each family enforces the shunning practices. One ex-Amish person told me, "I can meet my family on the same side of the street and they will walk by me as if I am a stranger." Some are still able to go home and the family members enjoy each other without talking about their differences. Other families may feel threatened by changes from the outside world and therefore reject their children and their newfound English families. Each family chooses either to nurture their bonds or to reject the family member.

All of the ex-Amish I interviewed have felt the effects of shunning. Often, those who have left find a contradiction between shunning and the expression of other religious principles. II Corinthians 2: 5-11, for example, states: "But if any one has caused pain, he has caused it not to me, but in some measure—not to put it too severely—to you all. For such a one this punishment by the majority is enough; so you should rather turn to forgive and comfort him, or he may be overwhelmed by excessive sorrow. So I beg you to reaffirm your love for him". Or in Matthew 7: 1-29—"Judge not, that you not be judged. . . "

Some of the statements ex-Amish made to me were: "What is the difference in their working outside the Amish community and our being on the outside of the community? That's living a double standard." "We are trying to live a good life on the outside. We are not any different than our Amish parents and relatives. The only difference is our clothing." "The more we put our faith in Christ and the more we read our Bible, the harder it is for us to understand the shunning." Many ex-Amish have found comfort and support in other churches where they now worship

It is not necessary for outsiders to understand the shunning practices. The Amish are like any other religious group. We are all given freedom of religion through the First Amendment of the Constitution of the United States.* The Amish have often said to me, "This is our way."

Just as we may not understand the logic of other cultures, we may not understand why the Amish believe in and practice the lifestyle and religion that they do. Despite what we may think, it is reassuring to know that the same laws that protect them protect our own religious beliefs and give us the freedom to be unique individuals in a democratic system.

I once made a remark in front of two Amish women that showed my ignorance concerning the Amish culture. They spoke to one another as if I were not present and yet in English for me to hear and understand, not in their Pennsylvania Dutch. "Oh, that's just Drucie," they said, exonerating me of fault. The Amish understand our confusion about their culture.

We who live near the Amish, as people looking in from the outside, may have misgivings about the Amish lifestyle and beliefs but living side-by-side with them has helped us gain knowledge and understanding of other ethnic groups.

In conclusion, it is appropriate to mention a comment from Doug Meikheim, a professor from the University of St. Thomas, who led an executive seminar group which toured the Amish community in Harmony. He stated that one of the positive views they gained from their tour was that, "Harmony, as a small town, has an example to offer the world. Two cultures existing at opposite ends of the poles have learned to exist in a harmonious atmosphere, not without problems but learning to solve problems within the law and community without wars and in a peaceful manner. Harmony is unique."*

Respect for Amish Roots

Leaving the community is not something Amish young people expect to do as they are growing up. Their decision to leave can create a great conflict between their sense of security in staying with a known way of life and their desire for a more modern, independent lifestyle. Andy, for example, was fifteen years old when he had his first thoughts of leaving. An older brother had left home at the age of twenty-one. At the present time there have been three boys who have left this family. A younger sister also left, but she returned when she became very ill; she died after a short illness.

On a summer night in June of 1990, an Englisher friend of Andy's came by at 10 P.M. after Andy's parents had gone to bed. The two friends had planned in advance for Andy's escape from the Amish community. He had no money when he left; however, his friend loaned Andy enough money to tide him over until he found work.

Andy soon found a job milking cows on a farm near Caledonia, Minnesota. He lived in the basement of his employers' home. They were kind to him and gave him room and board, plus a small wage. During the two years he lived with and worked for them, he went to school and got his GED. Andy would go home for visits, even though he felt

* U.S. Constitution, 1st Amendment, Bill of Rights.
* Phone interview with Douglas Meikheim, Adjunct professor, University of St. Thomas, St. Paul, MN, April, 1992.

unwanted. His parents, on the other hand, felt that he had abandoned them. All of them were suffering from the loss of their relationship.

For two more years, Andy remained on the Caledonia farm, but he missed his relationship with his family, and eventually he returned home. His return lasted two months. He could not fathom staying any longer. This time when he left, he moved into the small community of Canton, Minnesota, shared an apartment with friends, and again began milking cows for an English farmer. The first car Andy bought was a 1979 green Ford Thunderbird. Two weeks after buying the Thunderbird, he drove it into a tree. I told him that we didn't need to go into the details of his accident; however, he was quick to say, "No alcohol was involved. I had seven other people in the car and I was distracted. It was broad daylight and I was driving on a gravel road, I milked cows that same evening." He replaced the Thunderbird with a 1983 Oldsmobile Cutlass.

Andy quit milking cows when he found a job with Featherlite Trailers in Cresco, Iowa. Soon Andy had his own apartment in Canton. An older brother left home and moved into this apartment with him.

Many years have passed and Andy is now married and lives in Preston, Minnesota. He met his wife through a cousin who had also left the Amish community. The cousin was dating a girl who was a friend of Andy's future wife. His wife currently works as a secretary for Christ's Lutheran Church in Preston, although Andy and his wife are now members of the United Methodist church. They have three children, plus another child from a previous relationship of Andy's. He is very responsible toward all his children.

Since he left the Amish community, Andy has worked at various jobs. For twelve years he drove a semi tractor to 48 of the 50 states and Canada. He has owned a semi tractor for six years and has worked for AMPI, which is a private contractor.

Recently, he was hired by KEMPS, a company who delivers dairy products to grocery stores, schools, gas stations, and convenience stores. Having a delivery route has allowed him to be home with his family.

As Andy tries to maintain ties with his Amish family, he clearly feels the effects of the *meidung, or* shunning practices. He told me, "The more we put our faith in Christ and the more we read our Bible the more we can't understand this." However, Andy expressed a desire to pass the values his father taught him onto his children. He respects his Amish roots.

Part VIII

Other Stories

Stories

Accidents
Threshing Oats

The fall of the year is always busy on Amish farms, since harvesting and threshing must be done. This was also true of the fall of 2005, a time that would change a young boy's life forever.

Shocks of oats in a field.

Nine-year-old Enos was excited to be helping with the threshing. With his neighbor Levi and Levi's son, Enos arrived at the field where the rest of the work crew had gathered, ready to begin threshing the oats. Levi had even let Enos take the horses' reins to drive the wagon a short distance. When they came near the field, Levi took the reins again.

Once they were on the field, fourteen-year-old Eli began stacking the bundles of oats onto the flatbed of the wagon. Driving the hay wagon, Levi stood on the standard, a ladder-like frame that allows the driver to be higher than the stack of loose bundles and thus able to see to drive the draft horses. Enos stood on the standard next to Levi.

Everything was going well. The trained draft horses had always been easy to handle. The 'evener,' a wooden bar between the horses, kept them aligned so they pulled well together. On this day, however, what happened next would have

Stacking bundles of oats on a wagon, pulled by 2 gentle draft horses and guided by the man on the 'ladder-like standard.

118

sent the very best trained horses into a frenzy.

The wagon was less than half full of bundles to be hauled to the threshing machine, which, powered by a diesel engine and belt-driven, stood stationary on the driveway in front of the barn door.

The horses approached the end of a row of oats and were close to a gravel road. Suddenly, the front end of the ladder-like rack came loose and fell forward onto the horses. The horses—startled—went into a frenzy. Panic-stricken and out of control, they raced up a small ditch and onto the gravel road,

Levi fell with the wooden rack he was standing on and onto the horses. He was able to jump and roll away from the wagon soon after the horses got onto the road. Enos, however, who was standing next to Levi on the lower part of the wooden rack, lost his balance and fell forward between the evener and the horses. As he fell, he grabbed onto the first thing his hands came into contact with—the evener—and hung on fearing for his life.

Fourteen-year-old Eli's only thought was to get the horses under control. As the horses went up the knoll of the first hill, Eli jumped off the wagon and began running after the horses. He didn't see Enos nor did he realize Enos' predicament. Eli managed to grab the reins of one horse but not the other. Struggling against the weight and speed of the horse, he wasn't able to keep his hold on the reins. When he looked down, he saw Enos being dragged by the horses as they approached a second knoll.

The horses— still hitched to the wagon with the rack on their backs—were dragging Enos between them and the wagon. Enos felt the steel-rimmed wagon wheel brushing his right thigh as the horses dragged him on the gravel road. Afraid that he would be run over by the wagon, he didn't dare let go.

Desperate to help Enos, his father and the other threshers raced up the road with a horse and buggy. They searched the ditch for Enos, hoping that he had been thrown free. When they didn't find him, they realized how dire the situation was.

The horses slowed as they began to climb the second hill. Knowing this was a chance for Enos to get free before the horses could gain speed again, the men shouted to Enos,"Let go!"! He had to let go!

Finally, Enos found the courage to loosen his grip. The steel wheels of the wagon rolled past him. He had been dragged more than five-hundred feet on the gravel road. When his father and the other men reached him, they saw immediately that he was severely injured. One bared hip bone showed white through his shredded trousers and an area on his abdomen had a film-like covering.

Since the Amish have no phones, they went to an Englisher neighbor's home to call an ambulance. Enos was taken to Gunderson Lutheran Hospital in LaCrosse, Wisconsin, where he received treatment. Gravel was embedded in his abdomen and legs. He had to have skin grafting but miraculously no bones were broken. The second month after his accident, he was back in school. Enos recovered fully, although he did develop a hernia on his abdomen, which could be repaired by surgery. Since his accident, the family has moved to Staples, Minnesota.

Cutting Wood

His name, like his friend's, is also Enos. He too was nine-years-old when his accident happened. It was just before Thanksgiving in 2005.

Cooler weather was approaching, and the Amish needed to cut wood for their wood burning stoves. To cut the wood, they use a circular saw that is mounted on a platform and run by a gas engine, not electricity. The saw is belt-driven and attached to a drive shaft.

Young Enos was helping his older brother saw wood. He was wearing a pair of rubber gloves to protect his hands from the rough bark. Without thinking and on impulse, he grabbed hold of the spinning drive shaft with his right hand. The rubber glove adhered to the drive shaft and, as it turned, the shaft pulled his clothing into the mechanism. The engine shut down, but the twisted fabric had pulled Enos into the machinery and he was seriously hurt.

His brother knew Enos needed immediate help. Taking a short cut in back of their Amish home, he ran to the home of an English neighbor. There, he used the telephone to call 911 and ask for an ambulance. When the ambulance arrived, the EMT team made an assessment of Enos's injuries and had him air-lifted by helicopter to Gunderson Lutheran Hospital in LaCrosse, Wisconsin. He was severely injured and partially paralyzed.

At Gunderson Hospital, Enos was in intensive care for many weeks. Fearing for his life, his family never left his side. After months of medical treatment and therapy, he was able to return home on February 3, 2006.

Once he had returned home, he still required much care. He was confined to a wheelchair and had a catheter in his bladder. Periodically, he needed suctioning at his throat where a tracheotomy tube had been inserted, even though the tubing had been removed. He would sometimes cough or choke so hard that he needed a Heimlich maneuver to help him. He also needed physical therapy for an extended length of time.

Enos normally would not have been able to go back to school, but his eighteen-year-old sister was his teacher. To most teachers, his physical care would have been intimidating. Having nursed Enos at home, however, his sister knew his needs and willingly took care of them.

During the summer of 2006, Enos continued to recover. He had the tracheotomy opening closed, and his parents reported that he had gained feeling in his legs and could bend his right arm better, although his use of it was still limited. In August, he had a hydraulic lift, which put him into a standing position so that he could gain some strength back in his legs. Finally, during that summer, he was able to join his family doing something they all love to do——fishing.

Amish Grocery Store

When I arrived at the local Amish grocery store, two buggies were tied to the hitching post and one van was parked near the store. The horses and buggies continued to flow in and out of the yard while I waited to talk to my friend, the store's proprietor. It was interesting to see first-hand the activity the store generated. I knew the owner enjoyed the activity the store brings into her life and the chance it gives her to engage with friends in the community.

On this cloudy, gray and damp day, the weatherman was predicting snow and the store was especially busy with people stocking up on groceries before the storm hit.

Several patrons were waiting for Lovina's attention when a blond five-year-old—her great-nephew—came into the store, pulling a sled full of wood slabs for the store's wood burning stove. We all smiled at the great gusto and commotion of his entry. He was all business as he took one piece of wood after another and piled them in the wood box. When the sled—which was bigger than he was— was empty, he picked it up and carried it out of the store. Someone opened the door for him, and he made his exit with as much bustle and importance as his entry. He never said a word and never smiled. His focus was on his job.

Soon everyone had their orders filled and were on their way home.

Lovina's store, full of groceries, household items and goodies.

After Lovina had locked up the store, we went to her home. We were barely inside when her five- year-old great-nephew pulled in his sled and began to fill the wood box there, too. She thanked him and gave him a treat as he was leaving.

We sat down at the table with cups of tea, and Lovina told me the history of the store.

The Amish began moving here in 1974. Lovina's father, Old Dennis, had promised his friend—who was the first Amish family to purchase a farm near Canton in December of 1973—that he would get a farm in the area, too. He found land and a building site a quarter of a mile from Canton. His wife and daughter Lovina moved here with him. His daughter would eventually become the owner of the Amish grocery store.

First, however, Lovina was asked to teach the handful of children who were part of the community. She felt compelled to help out in anyway she could, and she was glad for the income the teaching position offered. She taught the children in a small bedroom off the sitting room of her parent's home. The following year, the community built a one-room schoolhouse and found another teacher to conduct classes.

As more Amish moved into the area, a grocery store was established on the back porch of Old Dennis' home in 1975 for the convenience of the Amish community. The store was small but sufficient for the large bulk items bought by the Amish families. Lovina became the manager of the grocery store, which existed for twenty years in the back of their home. In 1994 a new store was built, which is the one Lovina now runs.

Another way in which Lovina helps her community is by maintaining the history and records of the Amish who move into and out of the area. The records include marriages, births and deaths. She began keeping track of this information shortly after she moved here from Ohio.

A particular interest of hers is keeping the genealogy of Peter Hershberger—her great-great-great grandfather— updated. When she took over the genealogy, the family history she had covered were the years 1810 to 1969.

I asked her, "In your genealogy, what was the largest number in a family?"

"Twenty children born to one couple," she replied.

"Were there ever more than one or two spouses in a marriage?"

We looked for the answer to my question in the large volume of family history Lovina had placed on the table. We discovered that one man had three wives. With his first wife, who died in 1919, he had five children. He married his second wife two years later and they had eight children. Three years after this wife had also died, he married his third wife. They had seven children. Their last child was born after the mother's forty-second birthday.

Next, we looked up how many states Peter Hershberger's descendants had settled in. We came up with eleven: Missouri, Kentucky, Tennessee, Pennsylvania, Ohio, New York, Indiana, Maryland, Michigan, Wisconsin and Minnesota.

"How many countries does your genealogy cover?" I asked her.

She replied, "Germany, Holland, France and the Netherlands, also South America and Canada. It took three months before I heard from the relatives in South America."

I had to decline when Lovina asked me to join her for a hot meal of fish and bread. I had enjoyed our time together, but with the storm predictions for the evening hours, it was time for me to head home.

Amish Home for Sale on the Internet in 1999

The following events were related to me by Marc DeKeyrel and his wife, Heidi Ochtrup. They were living in Minneapolis and wanted to find a farm to buy. They began surfing the Internet, hoping to find farm property for sale between Minneapolis and Rochester, Minnesota. This is what they told me:

"We were both working our regular day jobs and growing vegetables on the side at a friend's farm. We sold our produce to customers through an arrangement called Community Supported Agriculture. (This is a subscription-based model. People buy a 'share' of the produce at a set price at the beginning of the season. They then receive a weekly delivery of produce throughout the growing season.)

"We enjoyed the business and wanted a farm of our own. We only needed ten acres to continue and expand the business. We also wanted to move to the country for a quieter lifestyle and felt it would be a good place to raise our three children.

"We began looking for a place between Rochester, Minnesota, and the Twin Cities. Everything we looked at in our price range with ten acres and a home was not very desirable. The houses on these properties either needed to be torn down or burned to the ground and rebuilt. We were getting discouraged.

"In December of 1999, I (Marc) was surfing the Internet when I came upon an interesting piece of property listed with Edina Realty Co. It was an Amish-owned farm of about forty acres near Harmony, Minnesota. The list price was $190,000. On the land were a house, barn, and the old Wilton Center School, which had been built in the 1900s. The listing intrigued us, but the farm was way out of our price range.

"Whoever was helping the Amish family list the property presented the farm— which had no modern conveniences—as a positive arrangement. It was the end of 1999 and nearing the close of the year. There was much concern about Y2K.*

"A full scale computer crash in 2000 was threatening to cause a collapse in society. The chaos this would cause was unconceivable. Anxious people were interested in finding a safe place to live.

"Many buyers were interested; however, people had trouble getting financing. The reason for this difficulty was because the typically Amish home had no furnace, no indoor bathroom facilities, and no plumbing. Water was pumped into the house via a pump-jack and only cold water was available. There was a large kitchen with a pantry but no cupboards. The house lacked most modern conveniences, including electricity.

---

* www.bizjournals.com/site

"The initial interest in the property faded and the price dropped to $169,000. We still could not afford to buy it, but we continued to dream about this particular piece of land.

"I had my father go look at the property, since he lived in the same area where the Amish farm was located. Dad told me, 'You don't want that farm. It doesn't have any of the modern conveniences and it'll take a lot to get it modernized.'

But we were still interested and decided to see it for ourselves. The day we went was a cold day and the farmyard had not been cleared of snow. We felt a little awkward as we parked on the road in front of the Amish home. We were used to showing our home and the realtors made sure we were gone whenever we had an open house. In this case the family would be present. We felt like intruders as we went to the house and knocked on the door. The Millers invited us into the house, and we liked the home and the farm.

"The farm wasn't selling and the price had come down again. We made a second visit and soon afterward we made an offer very close to their asking price. The only contingency to our purchasing the property was that we had to sell our home first.

Amish home with dry sink.

"A few days went by and then a week. The housing market was going wild, especially in the Twin Cities. It was not unusual for an offer to be made and then have counter offers and agreements reached within a few days.

"In our case, however, we understood that the cultural differences might slow down the purchasing process and make it take longer.

"Two more weeks went by—we still hadn't heard back on our original offer or been given a counter offer. When we called the realtor, we found

125

After purchasing the farm, the DeKeyrels heated the house with this gas furnace.

out the Millers had rejected our offer and taken their farm off the market. Our disappointment was indescribable!

"In the meantime we set about getting things in order for the sale of our home. We had an Open House, and thirty interested parties came to see our home. The next day we had three offers to buy our house and in fifteen minutes time, we had it sold.

"We kept looking for a place of our own but nothing interested us more than the Amish farmland we'd set our dreams on.

"Four weeks after we sold our home, we got an unexpected call from our realtor, who told us the Millers were ready to sell. They were wondering if we were still interested. Needless to say, we were!!

"Here we are seven years later. It has been a huge lifestyle change from city life to country life. We ended up putting in a new well and installing electricity into the house, but the home is basically the same. We did continue our vegetable business and added a host of different animals to the mix——chickens, broilers and 800 laying hens, pigs, goats, etc. We love the area and are happy in our Amish-built home."

At one point, the Millers did come back to visit their Amish families and included a visit to the DeKeyrel's farm. Mrs. Miller was surprised at the difference in the home since they'd left; however, when she looked up the stairwell and its bare walls she exclaimed, "Now that looks the same."

The Dekeyrels remodeled kitchen was kept simple and efficient.

Courtship, Singing, and Making Fry Pies

One winter day, I stopped at the home of Amish friends to purchase some eggs. The mother and her daughter were busy getting the noon meal ready. During our visit, Hannah, who was eighteen, told me her cousins and friends had been invited to their home to make fry pies. Never having heard of fry pies, I asked Hannah what they were. I was surprised and pleased when, instead of answering my question, Hannah said, "Would you like to come to see how they are made?"

Marion, her mother, also encouraged me to come. "You'll enjoy seeing how the fry pies are made. They have a very flakey crust with a filling."

"What kind of a filling do you use?" I asked.

"We use peach and raspberry but our favorite is apricot."

I knew I had a can of apricot pie filling on my pantry shelf. "Not only will I come, I'll bring a can of apricot pie filling."

When I arrived at the house on the day of the party, December 26th, Hannah greeted me with a welcoming smile. "You're just in time. We're about to get started. Mom had to take the horse and buggy to town early this morning because we forgot something, but now we're all set to go."

Besides Hannah, three other girls were there, ranging in age from sixteen to nineteen. All of them were pretty in their white prayer kapps and long dresses with matching bibs. One girl wore a dark green dress, while the other three wore varying shades of blue.

Taking off my coat, I sat on a long bench near the window and watched the girls wipe the table with sudsy hot water. When that was done, they placed their utensils, fillings, rolling pins and other necessary items on the white oilcloth covering the table. The way the table was placed, the girls could work on both sides of it. Rather than speaking in their first language of Pennsylvania Dutch, the girls were kind enough to use English so that I could join in the conversation.

Two of the girls, Beth and Helen, sprinkled flour on the oilcloth covering the table. Then they began rolling out the soft dough. After this was done, they made circles in the dough by using a cutting wheel to trim around a small saucer. Next, they placed the filling on one side of the circle and folded the dough over the filling to make a half moon pie. Standing at the stove, Ruth placed the filled pies into hot grease until they were light brown and flakey. Her cheeks became quite rosy as she worked over the hot stove. Hannah's job was to spoon a glaze over the hot fry pies. Her mother thought Hannah was

127

wasting the glaze by using too much, but Hannah pointed out that she had placed a pan under the cooling rack to catch the drippings so that she could reuse the glaze.

Making fry pies.

The kitchen became warmer and warmer, and soon all of the girls were as pink cheeked as Ruth.

Marion, Hannah's mother, said, "Two years ago we made 500 fry pies. That was too many at one time, even though we had many hands helping. I was tired before we were done but the others weren't."

"The boys came that day too," Hannah added. "While we girls were making fry pies they shot at clay pigeons. They had brought their rifles and took turns throwing the clay pigeons into the air and shooting at them."

The girls, Ruth, Beth, Helen and Hannah, laughed when I asked, "Which of the boys did the best in the competition?"

Ruth answered, "According to the boys—listening to them tell it— they all won the competition."

We heard the wheels of a buggy coming into the yard. Looking out the window, we saw Aunt Myra and Uncle Ezra arriving. Ezra tied the horse to the hitching post and headed for the furniture shop owned by Hannah's father. Myra came directly to the house. She was greeted with smiles and much activity.

When Aunt Myra sat on the bench next to me, she saw I was writing the recipe for fry pies. "Have you ever heard of an 'Adjective Letter'?" she asked me. I replied that I didn't know what it was, so Marion told Myra to show me by writing an Adjective Letter. In this type of letter, blank spaces are put where the adjectives are supposed to be.

After Myra had finished the letter, we took turns giving her adjectives. She put the adjectives we suggested in the blank spaces.

Hannah supplied the first adjective, which was "runny," Beth gave the next word "crazy." Helen's suggestion for the third adjective was "dirty," and Ruth, who was deep-fat frying the pies, gave the word "greasy." So the game continued, with the girls calling out descriptive words to fill in the blanks. We knew it would be a mixed up composition but that was the fun in creating it. Below is the finished Adjective Letter:

Hello _runny_ girls

Greetings to the_crazy_ fry pie girls. Hannah is _dirty_ glazing the _messy_ pies. Beth is rolling out _delicious_ pie dough and making _sticky_ raspberry fry pies. Helen is also _creamy_ rolling out _hot_ pie dough and putting _green_ raspberry filling on the _flaky_ dough, _licking_ them in half before _snowing_ the dough together around the edges. Ruth is _busy_ putting the _jolly_ fry pies into the _funny_ oil until they are _black_. Marion is _wiping_ getting a _muddy_ dinner ready. Drucie is _Sweetie_ & is sitting on the _pretty_ bench watching the _smelly_ girls making _red_ fry pies and asking the _old_ girls _rosy_ questions. Sometimes there are _belly_ laughs. We hope no one eats too many _yellow_ fry pies. It could cause a _stupid_ stomach.

The letter should have read:

Hello _young_ girls,

Greetings to the _happy_-fry pie girls. Hannah is _busy_ glazing the _wonderful_ fry pies. Beth is rolling out _soft_ pie dough and is making _delicious_ raspberry fry pies. Helen is also _enjoying_ rolling out _soft_ pie dough and putting _red_ raspberry filling on the _soft_ dough, _flipping_ them in half before _pressing_ the dough together around the edges. Ruth is _busy_ putting the _small_ fry pies into the _hot_ oil until they are _brown_. Marion is _cheerfully_ getting a _good_ dinner ready. Drucie is _interested_ & is sitting on the _long_ bench watching the _busy_ girls making _delicious_ fry pies and asking the _young_ girls _many_ questions. Sometimes there are _good_ laughs. We hope no one eats too many _delicious_ fry pies. It could cause a _sick_ stomach.

After the Adjective Letter was finished, our conversation changed to Sunday's church service and young people's singings.* Singings are held at the Amish home that hosts the church service, with services being held every other Sunday. The singings are in the evening at

---

* Songs are led by a song leader on church Sundays and taken from the 16th Century Ausbund. It was first published in1564. It is a collection of lyrics and verses only. The music itself is not printed but passed on orally. At Singings the songs are more lively but have no musical accompaniment.

7:30 or 8:00 P.M. Only the young people go to the singings. Generally, the Amish youth are sixteen when they are first allowed to attend. The singings last one to one-and-a half hours. Popcorn, coffee and a cold drink are served near the end of the evening.

The girls began talking about how many had been at Sunday's Christmas Day singing. The crowd had been small that evening— seven boys and eight girls. At some singings fifty or sixty young people might attend.

Since Christmas Day had been mentioned, I inquired what the girls had gotten as gifts from their boyfriends. Helen had received a food strainer of stainless steel, which had several attachments. Ruth had been given an oak shelf. Beth's gift was a set of eight blue glasses and Hannah's was a green dish. Green is her favorite color.

"Do the boys only see their girlfriends every other Sunday?" I asked. "Do you plan your dates?"

One of the girls replied, "Oh, we just happen to be at the same singing." All of them laughed when she said this.

"So you only see each other every other week when your church district has church?" I persisted. There was even more laughter at this question.

"There are another five church districts and other singings every week and we might accidentally be at the same one." Again there was laughter at this teasing remark.

A green glass dish.

Joining in the fun, I said, "I suppose your boyfriends just happen to take you home the long way".

"Drucie's not so dumb! "Aunt Myra exclaimed. "She was young once upon a time too!"

"This is getting interesting," Aunt Myra continued, "but you didn't ask the girls what they got the boys for Christmas."

A handmade chest of inlaid diamond cuts of cedar and walnut.

"I'll show you," Hannah offered. "I've got another one upstairs just like the one I gave him." She ran upstairs and returned with a locked treasure chest made of inlaid diamond cuts of cedar and walnut. Helen had also given her boyfriend a treasure chest of cedar. Both girls had handcrafted their gifts.

"I gave mine a kerosene lamp," Ruth chimed in.

Beth said, "I made a shirt for my boyfriend. It was the first one I ever made. I made it wider than my brother's and it fit"

"Did you get the button holes in the right way?" I asked. "I always had trouble putting those in."

"She had mom do the button holes for her."

Aunt Myra confessed she also had made mistakes with hand sewing button holes. "One time I put the button hole in on the wrong side."

After much laughter and good humor, all fifty fry pies were done. The girls began cleaning off the table, washing the dishes and putting away the utensils. The morning had gone by very fast, with laughter, fun and warm feelings of friendship.

Hannah's mother had been getting food ready for the noon meal while the fry pies were being made. Earlier in the morning, she had put a smoked chicken in the oven of the wood-burning stove. She had then made a delicious bread dressing from a mixture of canned chicken, potatoes, carrots and celery. Along with homemade wheat bread, there was also coleslaw made from finely cut cabbage mixed with a sweet dressing. Dessert was cherry cheesecake and, of course, fry pies.

After Peter and Ezra had joined us for the meal, we sat at the long harvest table, now ladened with delicious food. We bowed our heads in silent prayer and gratefully thanked God for His blessings, which had been many this day.

FRY PIE RECIPE

9 Cps cake flour	2 Tbs sugar	1 Tb salt	2 Cps water
Thick fruit filling	3 Cps shortening	Shortening for deep-fat frying	

Glaze:

4 lb.pwdr sugar	1 tsp vanilla ext
1/4 Cp cornstarch	1 1/4 Cps wm water

To make pies, combine flour, sugar, and salt in a large mixing bowl. Cut in shortening until pieces are the size of small peas. Add water, a little at a time, until the flour mixture is moistened. Form into four balls. Divide each ball into ten pieces and roll each piece into a circle topping one side of the circle with filling and then folding the circle in half. Crimp edges to seal. Heat shortening & fry a few pies at a time in deep fat until golden brown. Cool on wire racks. Meanwhile, in a large mixing bowl, combine all glaze ingredients until smooth. While the pies are still warm, spoon the glaze over the tops. Allow pies to drip on wire racks until cool. Yield: about 40 pies.

Honeymoon Cottage

The Amish community gives prime examples of living a simpler life without modern technology. Part of their lifestyle is also to make do using what is available and affordable. They know they often have to wait for and work for ways to improve their lives. The sharing of goals and working towards those goals gives a sense of accomplishment and brings their community into a closer relationship.

I have witnessed this several times throughout the years. Young people, for example, will live in houses that are set on skids. These serve as living sites until the they can obtain land, then the house will be moved on those skids. Sometimes a shed may be built first and serve as a home until a house can be built. Or, as in the instance related below, a garage may even serve as a home.

In December of 1999, a young Amish family—father, mother and three children— bought a building site that was part of Chuck and Marietta Dennstedts' farm auction sale. The site included a small house that Chuck and Marietta had lived in briefly after they were first married. The family moved into the house and lived there for six years. During this time, Chuck built a new garage on his adjoining property and offered the family his old one. Chuck and the Amish father worked with other Amish friends to move the garage to the other farm. They used a jack to raise the garage off its cement slab and put the building up on blocks. The garage was then loaded onto a trailer, and a tractor hauled the garage down the road to the Amish land, where it served as a storage shed.

After living in the small house for six years, the Amish family decided it was time to build a more Amish-style home suitable for their family. While the old house was being torn down and the new one built, the family needed a place to live. The garage became their temporary home. Since the garage had been moved off the cement slab on which it had been built, the Amish put in a wood

The garage on the left was turned into a home while the family built their new house. Later, The two buildings were connected by a passageway to make a large woodworking shop.

132

floor. They also added windows, wallboard and insulation. With the ingenuity, insight and love of a caring father and mother, the garage was soon transformed into a home.

The young mother invited Marietta to see the transformation that had taken place. Marietta said their former garage was turned into a lovely and comfortable home. Even though it was one large room, the Amish had used two large cupboards to create a bedroom wall. The bedroom had a double bed and a crib for the baby. The larger part of the room had daybeds along one wall for their other two children. Two comfortable rocking chairs, an old-fashioned clock, and a long table served as a living area. There was also a wood-burning stove with a reservoir for heating water, a dry sink and another cupboard.

The garage after the family moved out.

After the Amish family had moved into the garage, it was time to take down the small house in which they'd been living. Chuck was part of the crew that helped to tear down the old house. As they worked, Chuck teasingly remarked to the young father, "You know, this is Marietta's and my honeymoon cottage that we're tearing down." The Amish workers all laughed at Chuck's romantic description of what was left of the house. The crew worked hard and diligently, and soon the honeymoon cottage was torn down and set aflame, becoming just a memory of another time and place.

A hand-guided dredge, pulled by horses, is used to dig the basement and foundation of new Amish homes. The foundations are made of cement or cement blocks.

Eventually, the garage was transformed again into a finishing room for the Amish father's woodworking, where he makes fine furniture to provide a living for his family. A small passageway connects the two buildings, providing shelter from the cold, snow,

Canned goods on the cement shelf in the basement of the new house.

rain and wind. as he moves between them.

Laundry rooms are also often connected to homes with this same type of passage. Many times, an outhouse is then attached to the laundry room. This type of construction conveniently shuts out the unpleasant elements of the weather.

The new house was used for church before the family moved in.

Basements sometimes are built with cement shelves for preserving canned meats, vegetables, and fruits. Root cellars are also constructed for storing fresh vegetables from their gardens.

A church service was held in this new home in September, 2005, before furniture was added.

I was told a five bedroom Amish home can be built for approximately $55,000. This does not include plumbing, electricity, furnace, air conditioning, carpeting and modern kitchen conveniences.

The newly built home.

The Insight of a Child

As we adults often realize, children can be more observant and sensitive than their ages might indicate. This story about a small five-year-old Amish girl shows a sensitivity and caring attitude beyond her years.

Amish mothers usually deliver their babies at home with the help

134

of midwives. In this particular Amish home, a midwife delivered a handsome baby boy who looked normal in every way. Everyone assumed that his development, too, would be normal—it was not.

As he grew up, he could not speak and his only way of communicating was to make unintelligible, guttural sounds. He also showed no sign of any rational thought processes. The family took him to many doctors and clinics. At one time his parents believed that he had had lead poisoning. His birth had been long and hard, and I often wondered if he may not have gotten the oxygen he needed at the time he was born.

Physically, the boy appears to be normal. He still has the face of an angel and the innocence of a baby. The family continues to allow no one outside their home to care for him because they believe they know him and his needs best. His family members use kind firmness, consistency and gentleness in how they deal with their son and brother. The love the family gives to this child is undeniable and witnessed in the simplest of tasks. Every family member gives him great care and understanding.

One day while at the home of these Amish friends, I witnessed how even one of his youngest siblings had absorbed what she must do to take care of her brother. In preparation for doing fieldwork, the father and his other sons had harnessed their team of Belgium horses to a wagon inside the barn. The handicapped boy, then eight years of age, was standing in front of the barn's large open doors. (In the winter months the doors are shut; however during the warmer months these doors are left open.) He did not comprehend how dangerous it was that the horses were hitched up, ready to be driven out of the barn and he was in the way. His five-year-old sister saw him standing in imminent danger and went to him. She placed her small hand in his, then pulled him aside and out of danger. She kept hold of his hand until the huge horses were out of the barn and had been driven away.

When I saw this, I was in awe of how such a small girl had been aware of her brother's dangerous situation and knew what she had to do to protect him. I turned to her mother and asked, "Has she been told to take care of her brother?"

The mother's reply was as surprising to me as was what I'd just witnessed. She said, "We have never told her to watch out for him." The little girl's actions were a poignant reminder to me of how a family's everyday actions can influence their children and make them capable— or not capable— of much more than we than we realize.

Jordan's King Hussein and Queen Noor

King Hussein of Jordan suffered for several years with a cancer known as non-Hodgkin's Lymphoma. He came to the Mayo Clinic in Rochester, Minnesota, on a regular basis for medical treatment.

During his time in Rochester for one of his treatments, King Hussein and his wife Queen Noor decided to take their entourage to Harmony for an Amish tour. Of course—being a man of importance—this also included his bodyguards.

As is usual with our local Amish tours, Hussein and his wife stopped at many Old Order Amish homesteads where they could observe the lifestyle of these people.

One tour stop was at John's homestead and furniture shop. Suddenly, in the calm and quiet of the rural setting, an outburst of gunfire reverberated through the air. Hussein's bodyguards went on instant alert, immediately ready to protect their King.

The tour guide, Merlin Hoiness, nonchalantly assured Hussein and his body guards that they were in no danger and excused himself as he went into the furniture shop to talk to John.

The group on the tour didn't know what Merlin knew—that John was and is the instructor of gun and safety laws in the Amish community. John's teaching methods include letting the young Amish men target practice in the woods near his workshop. John said, "Merlin came in to tell me King Hussein and Queen Noor were with him on tour. When the bodyguards heard the gunshots they tensed up. Merlin told me we couldn't have the Amish young men shooting while the King and Queen were out here touring."

After King Hussein, Queen Noor, and the bodyguards heard John and Merlin's explanation, everyone relaxed and enjoyed the humor of the situation.

While touring the Amish community, the King and his escorts purchased baked goods and homemade bread at Amish homes. They acquired a special taste for Lydia Ann's homemade bread. The King and Queen even sent some of their people back to Harmony to purchase more of her bread. The bread was brought back to the Kahler Hotel in Rochester for the enjoyment of the

Kahler's employees, as well as King Hussein, Queen Noor, and their group.

King Hussein and Queen Noor's tour will always be remembered as a special event for both the Harmony and Amish communities.

A Late Night Visit

One hot summer night, my husband and I had gone to bed at our usual time, after the 10:30 PM news. Our bedroom was on the second floor of our home. Since we did not have central air conditioning, we had a window air-conditioner in the bedroom.

Later in the night, without our realizing it, our Amish neighbor and good friend came knocking loudly and frantically on our door. Old Order Amish do not have telephones, and he needed desperately to use our telephone. His son had to have medical help immediately. Asleep on the second story with the noise of the air conditioner running, we didn't hear his urgent knocking. When we did not respond, our neighbor tried the door and found it unlocked. He came into the house and placed a 911 call to the Harmony Emergency Medical Team.

We slept on, unaware of his dilemma, his entering our home, or his use of our telephone.

Early the next morning, our Amish friend returned to our house. He explained the situation of the night before. He and his son had been putting up loose hay in the heat of one of the hottest days of our summer, and his son had suffered heat stroke. Our neighbor handed my husband a freshly cleaned chicken and asked what he owed us for the use of our telephone. It was his way of apologizing for what he had done. We assured him that he was not to be concerned about using our telephone. His son was recuperating from the heat stroke, which was more important than his intrusion into our home and the cost of his use of our telephone.

Old Dennis

I first met the Amish man I knew as "Old Dennis" when he was in his 60s, which doesn't seem so "old" to me now. The longer I knew him, the more I came to admire him. To me, he embodied much of the goodness and wisdom of the Amish character and way of life. He was a man who carried his early lessons of responsibility and work ethics with him throughout his life. He was also a man of great skill, ingenuity and religious devotion. His stalwart adherence to the Amish beliefs and lifestyle formed his entire approach to life.

Born in 1915 in Hazelton, Iowa, Dennis was the oldest of three boys who lost their mother to the great pandemic flu that swept the country after World War I. He was three-years-old when she died. A few years later, his father remarried and had a second family.

This second marriage came about in a rather unusual way. Dennis's father's hired man instigated the relationship. Concerned for Dennis and his brothers, the hired man wrote to an Amish widow and signed the name of Dennis's father. The two began to correspond and eventually married.

As a boy, Dennis had an interest in gas and diesel engines of all kinds. His Old Order Amish community used only gas and diesel belt-driven engines—no electricity was allowed. Knowledge about such engines came very naturally to him. After he came home from a day at school, his choice would have been to go straight to work on engines; however, his father told him, "Dennis, you have other chores to do first." For Dennis, a sixth grade education was sufficient. He had an ingenuity that accompanied his talents, as well as common sense. As he grew older, his knowledge of mechanics and of how engines operated also grew.

Before moving to Canton, Minnesota, his address was Navarre, Ohio. On his property in Canton, there were two work buildings. In the larger building, he repaired small engines. During colder months, a wood-burning stove supplied heat so he could continue to work. Books and magazines on motors and mechanics were numerous in his shop. One magazine he subscribed to was *Popular Mechanics.*

Both the larger and the smaller buildings were full of machinery-related items. The smaller building was full of what I termed 'junk'. He smiled and corrected me, "It is not 'junk'." He used this collection of parts for replacement and making repairs. He almost always had parts someone could use. Besides motors, he also mended horse-drawn machinery, sometimes reusing parts of horse-drawn machinery he and others found in the Fillmore County area and other places in Minnesota where the Amish had settled. I am sure he often had to reinvent parts when they were not readily available.

Most of the parts that he had were sorted according to use, but to the unskilled eye it looked like 'junk'. When I asked him, "How do you keep track of what you have?" He smiled and pointed to his head, "I have a computer!"

Dennis's business also included working on motorized lawn mowers, both self-propelled and push mowers. Alongside his driveway, mowers were lined up, either waiting to be worked on or repaired and ready to be picked up. One time when I drove into his yard, I saw a motorcycle. Rather surprised to see a motorcycle in an Amish yard, I remarked to Dennis, "You have a motorcycle here?"

With a humorous glint in his eye, he replied, "It won't be here long." He never did say if he was working on it or not. Knowing Dennis, someone had brought the motorcycle to him for mechanical work. Both old and new motors were brought in for his skilled hands to work on.

Dennis did work on other modern items of our world, too. At one point, my husband and I took a string trimmer to him to be repaired. When I went to pick it up, I inquired, "How much do we owe you?"

He replied, "One dollar."

I said, "A dollar?! What did you do to fix it?"

With typical Dennis humor, he laughed, "I gave it a shot of penicillin."

The hours he spent in his shop were numerous; sometimes he forgot mealtime had arrived because of his involvement either in his work or talking to people who came to his shop. He loved to visit almost as much as he loved to work on engines.

Another of Dennis's enterprises was the buying and selling of steel. He sold the steel to others in both the Amish and English communities, plus the steel was used for the wheels and other parts of horse-drawn machinery and buggies.

One of the items he looked for were steel liners or tubs, like those used in old washing machines. These liners, when removed from the inside of the washing machines, had a large hole where the agitator had been. Dennis would take these liners to welders, who filled the holes with steel. The Amish would then use them as large caldrons or tubs. They would build a stone oven around the tubs and burn wood to heat water for washing clothes. Water boiled in this way was also used for the cold pack canning of meats, fruits and vegetables. The large caldrons created from the washing machine tubs would hold up to twenty or more quart jars.

The Amish and World War II

One of my conversations with Dennis centered on World War II. The Selective Service Act was established in 1940. This Act stated that men between the ages of eighteen and forty-four were eligible to be drafted into the military. The United States entered World War II on Dec. 8th, 1941, after the Japanese bombed Pearl Harbor. Since the

Amish were conscientious objectors because of religious beliefs, they would not go to war when drafted into the Armed Services. Dennis claimed that several of their young men were sent to prison with hardened criminals because the Amish were conscientious objectors.* Most of the Amish men, however, were given jobs doing volunteer work with the CPS (Civilian Public Service). This was a government-sponsored program designed to accommodate conscientious objectors. In the CPS, they did forestry, soil conservation or mental health work.

According to Dennis, many Amish objected to their boys being put into the CPS programs and sent far from home. Others of the Amish community reasoned that they should be satisfied because now their boys were not in prisons with hardened criminals

Some of these same people also reasoned that it was better if these young men were sent away from their own home areas to work. Their rationale for this was that some of the English neighbors might have had sons or other relatives who had been maimed or killed in the war and would resent the young Amish men who did not have to go and fight.

Along with certain Amish groups, some conservative Mennonites and Brethren congregations rejected the CPS as being too secular and too politically motivated. They did not like the term 'pacifists' and favored the concept of 'nonresistance'.

The Loss of a Son

Besides having lost his wife in 1979, Dennis also knew another of the deepest of human griefs when he lost a son in an accident that involved taking down a windmill.

Dennis had a son Levi, who grew into a strong young man. One time when Levi was trying to load a 250-pound pig onto a crate to take him to market, the pig had other ideas. Levi became frustrated at the pig's lack of cooperation. He finally caught the pig and lifted all 250 squealing pounds into the air and crammed the pig down into the crate.

On several occasions Dennis warned Levi not to misuse his strength, but Levi, being young, continually ignored this warning.

*www.swarthmore.edu

A windmill.

On one cold, frigid day, two Englishers and Levi—who was then 29 — were taking down a windmill by lowering it to the ground. They had left the wheel and the gear box on the windmill. As they slowly lowered the windmill with ropes, they lost their hold and the heavy windmill started crashing down. Levi grabbed hold of one of the windmill legs, trying to keep it balanced. He was thrown into the air like a rag doll. When he hit the frozen ground, he was already dead. Levi's tragic accident left behind a wife and three children.

Old Dennis himself was 84 when he passed away. Going to his wake was difficult for me. His sons, daughters and their spouses were all gathered at his home. On this sad day, I could still hear the voice of Dennis when we had talked about death many years before. I had told him how badly I was feeling at the loss of a close friend. His words to me were, "We should cry when there is a birth and rejoice at the time of death." I knew what he was saying. When there is a whole lifetime of living ahead, we know there will be many struggles. At the time of death, our struggling is over. Dennis's struggle was over on a hot summer's day in 1999.

What is the Importance of Living?

Knowing Dennis was a special experience and a memory that I will always treasure. In speaking to Dennis and others, I have often been told, "That's not our way," or "That's your way." This is how they identify the difference between our two worlds.

As I was talking to Dennis one day in his shop, I began thinking about our differences and wondered how the Amish felt about the way Englishers live. I asked him, "What do you think about me and my beliefs and living life the way I do?"

His answer surprised me and yet made sense. "I only know this way of life," he told me, "and you only know your way of life." His words were a wise way of saying that it was not up to him or me to make a final decision as to what is the 'right way' to live.

In an article she wrote, Mary T, Bell* captured Dennis in his own words: 'When I asked him 'What is really important?" He said, "Your soul."

Old Dennis's Auction

Warren Deters* heard of Dennis's death and knew he would be missed by those who knew him.

*Mary T. Bell, 'Vignettes,' *Fillmore County Journal*, December 8, 1997, p. 20.
*Warren Deters is a retired farm equipment dealer, a collector of 'Steel Wheel Era' farm machinery, 'Rusty Tractors and unique junk.'

He read of the upcoming auction and recalled 'The American Thresherman' magazine. He made the trip to Canton with one thing in mind, to purchase the magazine.

The bid went to $100 before the other bidder gave up bidding. After the bidding was done, the two gentlemen had a conversation in which the second bidder confessed, "My wife would not have been happy with me had I come home with a magazine I'd paid over $100 for."

Now 'The American Thresherman is over 100 years old and in the hands of a person who appreciates this magazine on old steam engines.

It is ironic how this particular magazine brought these two men, Dennis and Warren, together. Their shared interests and 'The American Thresherman' magazine made a minute meeting into a memorable moment in time.

Trust and Horse Sense

Early in life, many young boys show an innate talent for particular trades, such as woodworking or machinery. Others may show a knack for handling and understanding animals. Joe was one of these youths. From an early age, he had an interest in horses—those used for fieldwork and those used for buggies and riding. He learned to train horses, not from books, but from watching his elders train the field horses. An interest and love for horses was born in him. He could sense a horse's needs and knew how to read a horse's responses. By the age of thirteen, Joe knew that he wanted to learn the techniques of training horses. His connection to horses came as naturally as breathing to him.

Marcy was the first horse Joe trained. The mare had never been ridden, and Joe's inexperience was sometimes a problem when it came to training her. He enlisted the help of one of his six brothers, Mose. At the time, Mose was ten-years-old and took his older brother very seriously. He would do whatever Joe told him to do, with no questions asked. Both boys were anxious for the adventure of training Marcy and the fun they would have riding her.

Their first step in training Marcy was to place a small saddle on her. She had never been trained to a bucking belt or to the cinch.

Since Joe was bigger and stronger than his younger brother, he knew that he had to be the one to hang onto the long rope tied to Marcy as they trained her. He hoped he could hang onto the rope and control the horse if she began bucking. He told Mose to get into the saddle on Marcy's back and grab onto the saddle horn. Mose did as his brother told him and got up on the horse's back. Joe's only other instruction to Mose was "Hang on!" Mose hung on as hard as he could. Luckily, Marcy was cooperative and didn't buck him off. The memory of their adventure and inexperience still brings back smiles and laughter to Joe and Mose. They realize now how lucky they were that Marcy was a mellow horse.

Marcy was eventually used for driving as well as for riding.

Another horse Joe trained was Beretta, a family horse. The relationship that developed between horse and rider was an easy one of trust and enjoyment. Beretta liked to gallop down country roads and into wooded areas as much as Joe did. When he hunted squirrel, rabbit or possum, Beretta was like his hunting partner. She became used to the sound of his rifle and maneuvered her speed and body in a way that made their prey an easy target. Beretta could see when Joe brought his gun forward, aiming at his prey. She slowed or stopped, turning her head to the right, with her body at just the right angle. Beretta and Joe worked like a team, blending the horse's intuition and his rider's coordination.

The Dream of Owning and Training a Horse

While he trained his family's horses, Joe dreamed of owning a horse of his own. When he was eighteen, he read an advertisement about a colt for sale in Lanesboro. His father told him to go look at the colt, which belonged to a farmer who had several horses. When Joe first laid eyes on Ranger, he knew this was the horse for him. Ranger's colorings was just what he wanted, a black horse with a white blaze down his nose.

His father purchased the nine-month-old colt for $150, plus the added fee of $10 for trucking. Joe had the horse of his dreams.

The first few months Joe went easy with Ranger, spending as much time as he could with the colt and earning his trust. One of the techniques Joe used to get the colt accustomed to his touch was to rub him down. He also picked up Ranger's feet periodically, which helped to prepare the horse for the time his hooves would need trimming and shoeing. When Joe finally put a lead rope on Ranger, he took it well with no problems. The horse took to the halter and small saddle with the same ease as he did the lead rope.

Soon Ranger was following Joe around the farm without a lead rope, obeying small commands that Joe gave in his native German. When he and Beretta went riding, Joe began to take along the yearling.* He put a lead rope on Ranger and tied the rope to Beretta's

Ranger standing in the barn doorway, untied.

saddle horn. When hunting season arrived, Joe decided to include Ranger, who was now fourteen months old. Once again, he tied the lead rope to Beretta's saddle horn. On his first hunt, Ranger flinched when he heard the sound of Joe's rifle, but otherwise he did fine. Joe continued to take Ranger hunting and, after the season was over, he realized that Ranger had come a long way in his training,

The training techniques came together more quickly after Ranger was two years old. Joe would go into the barn to Ranger's stall, open the gate and tell Ranger to come. The stallion would follow Joe out of the stall, then stand still while Joe put the halter and saddle on him.

Joe began riding Ranger for short distances. He was careful, knowing his weight would be too much for the young horse, which needed time to build muscle before he was ridden much. Ranger trained well, never bucking or balking. Joe continued to talk to Ranger constantly during all of his training. He soon had Ranger trained to pull wagons and buggies. The horse proved his stability and patience both in dealing with highway traffic and in town while he waited, tied to a hitching post, for his master

Proof of a Well Trained Horse

Ranger often showed how well trained he was. At one point, Joe left Ranger tied to a tree for three hours. When Joe returned, he found Ranger thirty yards from where he had been tied, his strap broken. He could only guess what had happened. "It had grown dark and something must have spooked him. In jerking and pulling against the strap, the stallion must have snapped it. He was probably confused when I didn't show up to retrieve him, but he stayed there even though

---

* Webster's Dictionary- 'a yearling is an animal that is one year old or has not completed its second year.'

he was loose, until I came back for him."

Another time while Ranger was still a stallion, Joe rode him to a picnic. When they arrived, Ranger was not tied up but left rein free. The people could not believe Ranger stayed where Joe left him, even though there

Ranger walking free, with no restraints.

were mares around. Later Ranger wandered near an area where the children were eating and playing. Joe saw this, went over and without touching Ranger or taking hold of his neck rein, told Ranger to come with him. The stallion followed him to a grassy area where he grazed until it was time to leave.

Joe also rode Ranger bareback or with a saddle and no bridle. Ranger was so well trained that Joe could direct him by command while riding him. This is unique. Most riders use their knees to signal a horse to turn if there are no neck reins.

When Joe taught Ranger to lie down, it took only three times before all Joe had to do was touch him and issue the command. The horse's lying down became a laughing matter because Ranger would never lie on gravel, only on grass. Ranger knew his comfort level.

Ranger laying down, by command.

Ranger proved to be perfectly trained when confronted with different types of terrain—steep hills, bluffs, woods, streams and rivers. At one time on a trail ride in Forestville State Park, Joe stopped for a rest between a 70' cliff and the river; he removed Ranger's bridle. The stallion made no attempt to run off and paid no attention to the other horses in the area. He went off by himself to eat grass and drink from the river.

Joe even trained his dog, a rat terrier, to ride on Ranger's back when they went hunting. The dog rode behind Joe, who was riding bareback on Ranger. If Joe got off Ranger, the terrier stood up on Ranger's back until Joe returned. The small terrier served a purpose; he was good at treeing squirrels and chasing down rabbits. What a comical sight to see the three companions—horse, dog and man—out on a hunt.

As a boy, Joe had always dreamed of owning a horse and training it. Now as a young man he was using his experience with his family's horses and had learned that it was crucial to first establish a horse's trust before he started the training. The mutual trust between Ranger and Joe show how a horse and man can learn the mind and the will of each other. Their close companionship was the culmination of Joe's dream.

Training Techniques

Now 23, Joe has continued to train horses for both Amish and English. His brother Mose is nineteen and has continued to help Joe train horses. A younger brother Toby is also enjoying the adventure of taming and training horses.

A unique technique they have to train a horse to noise is that of a collar which has two jugs filled with rocks attached to it. The more a horse moves, the more noise the rocks make. They also use plastic bags (like grocery store bags.) They tie these to the harness with rings. When the wind catches these plastic bags, they make a loud rippling and slapping noise.

To give a horse respect for the cinch or bucking belt, the trainers use a cotton rope so there are no rope marks left on the horse. They place the bucking strap or the cotton rope around the horse's belly but up high on its front flank, making the belt snug. The strap or rope is moved back on the belly all along the back of the horse until it is by the horse's back legs. Joe's advice in using this technique is, "Don't leave the bucking strap or cinch hang down. Keep it snug but not tight. The horse will never get used to a firm belt if you leave it loose. The cinch will get tighter going downhill and the horse may go wild. This is why many riders get bucked off. "This technique also helps to train a horse for the time a branch might touch its back."It takes the buck out of them," Joe says.

Joe and Mose now charge a fee of $300 a month to train a horse for riding and $350 a month to train a horse for both riding and driving.

A New Adventure

Besides training horses, Joe is also contracted to make furniture at the Countryside Furniture Shop* and helps at home on the farm. During all his time working, his goal has been to save towards a place of his own.

Bake goods on display and for sale.

He achieved his goal in 2006 when he purchased a building site with a few acres just off Highway 52 between Canton and Harmony, Minnesota. A bakeshop, craft shop and farmers market have been in business on this farm since 2002. Joe is not yet married, but he has three cousins who will take care of the farmers market for him. He will also have a furniture shop eventually. The house on the farmstead is only two years old. With his new responsibilities, he will not have time to train horses. His brothers may eventually take over the horse training.

Joe is representative of the young Amish men and women who are brought up in families with good work ethnics, a respect for others, and a chance to develop their own skills. Their initiative and ambition maintains the vibrancy underlying the traditional Amish lifestyle.

When an Amish Family Moves

As I drove down Highway 52 on a dark February evening, I had a hard time knowing which road led to the Amish homestead where I had an appointment. Since the Amish don't use electricity, there were no yard lights, nor were there house lights showing through the windows of the home. They do use kerosene lamps, but the light from these is filtered through the dark navy blue curtains that cover the windows.

Of course—you might have guessed—I missed the driveway. I turned the car around at the next Englisher's driveway. Retracing my route, I watched more carefully so that I would not miss the Amish home again.

The purpose of my visit was to discuss the family's upcoming move

*The Countryside Furniture Shop is the one visited by King Hussein and Queen Noor when they came to Harmony and took an Amish Tour.

Glass kerosene lamp.

to Pennsylvania. As I drove into the darkness of the farmyard, I saw muted yellow light shining through the windowpanes of the furniture shop.

With no yard lights to help me see in the dark, I used a flashlight to guide me to the front door of the house. The home—a large one with a wide, long open porch—had been built two years ago. When Anna, the Amish housewife, saw me at the door, she greeted me warmly. She was expecting me, since earlier in the week I had arranged for this time to see them.

Anna ushered me into the white painted kitchen. Typical of Amish homes, the oak floors were swept clean, and the hutches, dry sink, and free-standing cupboards* were also all made of oak. A long harvest table was covered with a white oilcloth. The black wood-burning stove had been polished so that it glistened.

The house was warm, comfortable and immaculately clean. Eli and Anna's five children were all seated in the large living room. Ranging in ages from thirteen to eighteen, some of them had been reading books before my arrival interrupted them. It seemed to me a good way for a family to spend an evening—no television, curled up with a good book, surrounded by family. A puppy was sleeping near the wood-burning stove, while an adult dog slept peacefully in a box nearby.

Woodburning cookstove.

When I asked the children what they were reading, the two boys responded by showing me the covers of their books. They were reading selections from *The Hardy Boys* series.

"The girls are reading *The Midnight Test*," Anna explained. "It's a story about a young man who wants to become a member of a club,

---

* The Amish do not build cupboards into their homes, and when they purchase a house with modern, built-in cupboards, they remove them. Hutches and free-standing cupboards are more convenient, since the Amish tend to move frequently to other areas and begin new communities.

148

but he first has to be accepted by the other club members. His acceptance proves to be a test of his character."

Comfortable chairs for reading.

"Aren't you still in school?" I asked the youngest boy. He was thirteen and in the eighth grade. His brother and sisters were no longer in school, since they had completed eighth grade. "You'll have to finish in a new school. How will you feel about that?"

"I'll be done with school before I leave."

Anna explained, "We're moving March 7th, so he's taking his tests early. He's a good pupil. He'll be able to finish school before we move. We thought it would be better for him and us this way. There will be so much to do." The boy's aunt was his teacher, and she had assured the boy and his parents that he was capable of finishing his schooling early.

Eli came into the house from his workshop. He joined us after he had washed his face and hands.

"What town will you be living near in Pennsylvania?" I asked him.

"Arronsburg. The population is 485. We both have family living there. Anna has a sister and two brothers in the area and I have a brother. My brother is married to Anna's sister."

Anna joined in, "There are two Amish church districts, with about fifteen to seventeen families in each district."

When I asked if they had bought a home in Pennsylvania, Eli answered, "We bought a seventeen-acre farmstead from the bishop of our church. It's bare land. A house, barn and woodworking shop will have to be built after we move. We've hired a local Amish contractor. I hope we can get the new buildings finished in six months. I don't know if it can be done."

One of the customs of the Amish is that many in the community volunteer to help raise a house and a barn. With such a large, willing work crew, I knew it was very possible that the three buildings could be raised within Eli's timeline.

"Where will you live while all this is being built?"

"Anna's brother has offered to let us live in their new home with them.

Kerosene lamp.

"My brother's family has been living in the basement, waiting until the main floors of their house were done," Anna explained. "We told them we'd be satisfied to rent the basement until our house was built but they wouldn't let us do that. They said, 'Our children are younger and we're settled in the basement for now, so you move up into the house'."

It struck me how much activity there would be in such a full house, with Eli and Anna's five children and her brother's seven children.

"Will you be making furniture there?" I asked Eli.

"There's a market for furniture and not many furniture craftsmen in the area. Our sons will have work there, too, probably building sheds and making pallets."

Like most young people, Eli and Anna's children had mixed emotions about the move. Leaving friends behind is never easy.

The oldest son had just recently been seeing a young girl in the community and he was naturally conflicted about moving so far away from her. Writing letters was one way for them to keep in touch, and the family would also come back to visit parents and other family members still living in Minnesota.

For the past two years on their home site, Eli's family had run a farmer's market, bakeshop and craft shop for tourists. They made the baked goods in a bakehouse that was not connected to the house. The large wood-burning oven, which held 40 loaves of bread, was left behind for the next owner.

The huge oven in the bakeshop.

Leaving their family-run business was another change for the family.

Moving Day: March 8th

Many relatives and friends came to help Eli and Anna move. They brought food as well, which provided a meal for everyone. The packing began with the contents of the house being taken outside to where a large trailer was parked. The organizing began and decisions were made as to what should be placed where in the trailer. One or two men took the responsibility for packing and organizing the trailer, while others gathered the family's belongings together and packed them for the move. The men who acted as overseers were very efficient.

150

A local trucker moved the livestock—four horses, one cow and a heifer. The dogs went with the livestock. The shop machines, furniture, buggies, and other equipment were moved in the 58 foot trailer hired especially for this purpose.

The family traveled by Amtrak to their new home in Pennsylvania. The children were excited about the ride, as they had never traveled by train before.

Five Months Later

Eli's plan to have everything built in six months was nearing completion. A large shed was moved onto the property to serve as a workshop for Eli. Eli and Anna's family moved into their new house on November 18th. A barn-raising was held on December 16th. Thirty-five families, which included sixty-eight men, helped to build the barn. Eli had thought the barn might take sixteen days to complete, but as it turned out, the barn roof was on by 11:30 of the first day.

Both of their sons found work, one building small sheds and the other working in a sawmill. Before she and Eli were married, Anna had taught school for one year. In Pennsylvania, she again became a teacher at Quarry School. She started with five first graders and twenty pupils in the other grades. Her school was one of two in their Amish community. The other school, Bower Hollow, had 23 pupils.

Facts About The Amish of Harmony
(S.E. Minnesota area)

1. Amish Mennonite roots date back to the 1500s in Zurich, Switzerland.

2. Menno Simons, a Catholic priest from Holland, joined the Anabaptist movement in 1536.

3. The Amish broke away from their Mennonite roots in 1693. Jacob Amman was their founder and was a Swiss Mennonite bishop.

4. The Amish believe in adult baptism (Anabaptists) and a life of self-denial, renouncing the modern world and its temptations and lures.

5. This group in Southeastern Minnesota is known as "Old Order," meaning least progressive. They have no automobiles or tractors, and no electricity. The first Amish settling here were from Wayne County, Ohio. (They have migrated here from Canada, Ohio, New York, Michigan and Pennsylvania.)

6. There are 6 church districts, with one bishop, a deacon, and two ministers for each church district.

7. Amish do not have to use the colored slow-moving vehicle sign on their buggies and wagons, believing they would be putting their faith in a sign rather than God. The courts ruled that, for religious reasons, Amish do not have to use the SMV sign or any alternative.

8. Bishops, ministers, and deacons are not ordained in the modern world's terms of ordination, (having a certificate of ordination). They are ordained by God and are commissioned by God to serve and therefore do not get paid.

9. Church, baptism, courtship, weddings, births, and funerals take place in the homes.

10. The Amish call all non-Amish "English".

11. Amish homes have beautiful Amish-made furniture.

12. Homes have bare floors and dark curtains of navy blue.

13. Only cold running water is found in Amish homes. It is heated in and on wood burning cook stoves for dishwashing, bathing, and washing clothes.

14. Almost all Amish women sew quilted items or make crafts to sell. This helps to supplement the farm income.

15. The first farm was sold to the Amish in December of 1973 and the family moved onto the farm in March of 1974.

16. Some Amish farms are only thirty to forty acres, but plat maps show the average farm size to be about eighty acres.

17. Most Amish families who farm, milk cows and sell grade 'B' milk in milk cans. This milk is used for dried milk and cheese.

18. Springs, circulating well water, and block ice (ice houses) are used for refrigeration and cooling milk. Therefore, the Amish smoke and can meats, vegetables, and fruits.

19. Amish normally stay on standard time. A few may have their time set for daylight savings time.

20. The Amish have wide doors on their barns because horse-drawn manure spreaders can be pulled straight through.

21. The Amish help one another thresh grain, fill silos, and raise buildings, (which they call frolics: barn frolic or barnraising, shed frolic, house frolic, depending on what building is being built).

22. Grain is cut with a horse-drawn grainbinder and put into shocks. A threshing crew works to bring in the grain and uses a threshing machine which sits in the barn or at the entry to the barn. It is belt-driven by a stationary engine.

23. Silage is cut with a horse-drawn corn binder. Silo filling crews exchange work or the corn is shocked and fed in bundles or shredded.

24. Corn is picked by hand (quite often by family members), then shoveled into corn cribs. Some Amish grind their corn and blow it into small silos with a stationary engine.

25. A corn shredder is used to remove corn from shocks and to shred the fodder and blow it into the barn or into a pile.

26. Husking bees, butchering bees, quilting bees and building frolics are considered social gatherings to accomplish and share work-related jobs.

27. All machinery has steel wheels.

28. There are 10 one-room schools where 1st to 8th grade is taught.

29. Teachers are 8th grade-educated.

30. The Amish believe in no graven images and base this belief on the 2nd commandment (Deut 5:8). Therefore there are no faces on dolls, no mirrors in homes (except for a small mirror for shaving), and no cameras or pictures. **They prefer no pictures of any kind.**

31. The Amish speak Low German/Pennsylvania Dutch in their homes and learn English only after they attend school.

32. Dress styles and home furnishings are identical within the group, promoting sameness and eliminating the symbols of fashion and material wealth.

33. Woodburning stoves are used for cooking and heating. Amish homes have no central heating systems.

34. They use horses to farm and for local travel.

35. Care for aged relatives is within the home on the same farm site as their children.

36. Some statistics (from 2008) since settling here in 1974:
    120 families;
    856 babies born;
    45 deaths since 1979;
    98 have left since 1987;
    70 families have left this area for other Amish Communities;
    10 schools (5 new schools built since 1974. The Vale school rebuilt);   Amish are located in 28 states and Canada.

Glossary

(Taken from *20 Most Asked Questions about the Amish and Mennonites,* by Merle and Phyllis Good, Lancaster PA, Good Books, 1979, pages 86-89. This is a very good resource book.)

Alternative Service - Various service projects administered by the church that fulfill government draft obligations yet do not violate church members' peace positions.

Amish Aid Society - An organization built on the principle of mutual aid. Church members pay annually into a reserve that is then available when disaster strikes a member.

Anabaptist - This is the nickname meaning "rebaptizer," given to the radical group of "Brethren" during the Protestant Reformation who advocated adult baptism. They believed the church should be a group of voluntary adults, baptized upon confession of faith.

Ausbund - The hymnal used by many Old Order groups, first published in Europe in 1564. It is a collection of lyrics and verses only; tunes are not printed but transmitted orally.

Ban - The practice of excommunication used as a means of keeping the church pure. The ban, based on I Corinthians 5:11, takes many forms, from members being refused communion to having other members not eat with them, visit, or do business with them. The ban is one of the issues over which the Amish and Mennonites split in 1693. The practice is designed to bring a member back into fellowship.

Barnraising - It is the practice of rebuilding with volunteer labor a barn that has been destroyed. Amish and Mennonite men gather for a day of work and socializing to build the bulk of the structure.

Bishop - This is a man ordained overseer of several congregations within a church district. His role is to coordinate leadership and decision making as well as to officiate at communion, weddings and funerals.

Broadfall Trousers - A style of trousers worn by many Old Order Amish men. Instead of a front zipper has a broad flap of cloth that is buttoned shut.

Budget (The) - A weekly paper that carries news of Old Order Amish communities across North America. Through its regular correspondents, it serves as an effective contact among the scattered groups.

Buggy - The horse-drawn carriage used for transportation by many Old Order Amish and some Old Order Mennonites. Although specific styles vary from community to community, buggies reflect a common commitment to simplicity and suspicion toward technology held by those who use them.

Cape – This is an additional piece of material that fits over the waist of an Amish dress. Worn by most Old Orders and many "conservative" women, it is designed for modesty.

Diary (The) - The only Old Order Amish magazine published in Lancaster County. A monthly, it records births, deaths, weddings, weather and farm reports for many eastern Amish communities, and usually includes a historical feature.

Eck – It is special corner table in the living room where the Old Order Amish bridal party sits to eat following the wedding.

Grossdadi House - The extension added to a home when a married child takes over the farm. Parents move into the new smaller section; the young, growing family occupies the large original part.

Martyrs Mirror - The large book of stories of Anabaptist martyrs, originally published in 1660. Full of graphic accounts of Christians dying for their faith, a copy is found in most Old Order homes and many modern ones.

Martyrs Synod – This is a gathering of early Anabaptists (1527) who laid plans for evangelizing Bavaria. Many were killed as they carried out their commissions.

Mennonite Central Committee - The inter-Mennonite relief organization is a committee that supplies food, clothing, community development workers, and financial aid overseas and throughout North America.

Mennonite Disaster Service - A network of grassroots volunteers of Amish and Mennonite men, women, and youth—across North America who come together during national or local disasters to clean up and rebuild.

Modern - A descriptive term used by the authors to designate those among the Mennonites and Amish who are more influenced in their primary decision making by what the larger society thinks than by what their faith fellowship believes.

Nonconformity - A belief that Christians are different from the world. These groups have given the concept expression in a variety of ways—distinctive dress styles, modes of transportation, wariness toward technology, living peaceably with all, advocating justice and the ethic of love.

Nonresistance - Love in practice; the ideal of returning good for evil, taught by Christ. Its practical expression means refusing to participate in any war, protesting class and racial discrimination, and for some protesting nuclear danger and world hunger. It is a peaceful approach to life that has also meant, for many, refusing to file law suits, participate in labor unions, or express anger.

Old Order - A descriptive term used by the authors to designate those among the Amish and Mennonites who take their cues for decision making primarily from their faith fellowship (instead of the larger world.)

Pathway Publishers - An Old Order Amish publishing house in Aylmer, Ontario, that publishes three monthly inspirational magazines; Family Life, Young Companion, and Blackboard Bulletin. In addition they publish schoolbooks (for Old Order schools), story books, adult instructional books, cookbooks, and some historical books in German.

Prayer Veiling – This is the head covering worn by women when "praying or prophesying;" an interpretation of I Corinthians 11.

Priesthood Of All Believers - The Biblical concept that within the church each member is responsible to counsel, discipline and support all other members. Although leaders are believed to be ordained of God, they are selected from the laity and act as servants of the church.

"Published" – This is the announcement of an Amish couple's plans to marry. The announcement is made by a bishop during a Sunday morning service.

"The Quiet In The Land" - Name given to Anabaptist groups as the movement settled down and many members fled to rural areas.

Schleitheim Confession Of Faith - The brotherly agreement arrived at by divergent Anabaptist groups, scattered across Europe, in 1527. It is often credited with unifying the brotherhood sufficiently to save the movement.

Shunning - An expression of the ban in which members do not keep company with an offending member who has fallen out of fellowship.

Steel-wheeled Tractors – This type of tractor and wheels are used by some Old Order farmers for field work. The steel wheels remove the temptation to use the tractor for transportation on the road.

Voluntary Service - Church administered projects that allow members to offer from three months to two years of their time for service overseas or at home, without pay.

Bibliography

Periodicals and Newspapers

"Amish have become main tourist attraction", Rochester Post Bulletin, Dec. 27, 1987

Bell, Mary T., *"Special Person Special Day", Fillmore County Journal,* Dec. 8, 1997

Capelle, Aleta, *"Innovative ideas are attracting new tourist interest in Harmony,"* Rochester Post Bulletin, Jan. 24, 1987

The Budget, a weekly paper serving the Amish and Mennonite communities throughout the Americas, published in Sugar Creek, Ohio, Sugar Creek Budget Publishers Inc.

Hansel, Jeff, *"Amish fearful of polio",* Rochester Post Bulletin, Oct. 19, 1005

"Harmony Amish farm tour set", Rochester Post Bulletin, Oct. 9, 1986

"Local woman serves others through alternative medicine", Fillmore County Journal, Feb. 16, 2007

Marshall, Bruce, *"Amish near Harmony open their doors"*, Rochester Post Bulletin, Oct. 13, 1986

Milne, Drucilla, *"The Amish Celebrate Christmas Simply"*, Fillmore County Journal, Dec. 19, 2005

Ode, Carson, *"Old Barn Memories",* Pamphlet, 1991

Severson, Harold, *"Amish lifestyle interest's visitors from around world"*, Rochester Post Bulletin, Dec. 5, 1987

Torgrimson, John, *"Local health officials inform Amish about polio",* Fillmore County Journal Oct. 24, 2005

"Uneasy neighbors", Minneapolis Star Tribune, Dec. 26, 1988

Vollmar, Alice, *"Life Among the Amish"*, MINNESOTA CALLS, Nov/Dec. 1992

Books read/or used as Resource Material

Allee, John Gage, compiler, *Webster's Encyclopedia of Dictionaries,* Ottenheimer Publishers, New American Edition, 1981

Dawley, Richard Lee, *Amish in Wisconsin.* Published by Amish Insight

Dummelow, Rev. R. *The One Volume Bible Commentary,* MacMillan, New York, 1936

Farm and Home Plat and Directory, Fillmore County, MN Belmond, IA, Farm and Home Publishers, 1991- 2007

Fisher, Sara E. and Rachel K. Stahl, *The Amish School.* Lancaster, PA, Good Books, 1986

Garrett, Ruth Irene with Rick Farrant, *Crossing Over-One woman's Escape from Amish Life,* Harper San Francisco

Good, Merle and Phyllis, *20 Most Asked Questions about the Amish and Mennonites.* Lancaster, PA, Good Books, 1979

Good, Merle, *Who Are The Amish?* Lancaster, PA, Good Books, 1985

Grolier Universal Encyclopedia, NY, Grolier Incorporated, 1965, Vol. 3.

Hostetler, John A., *Amish Society.* Baltimore, MD, Johns Hopkins University Press, 1968

Hostetler, John A., *Amish Life.* Scottsdale, PA, Herald Press, 1959

Kaiser, Grace H., *Dr. Frau.* Lancaster, PA, Good Books, 1986

Kloss, Jethro, *Back to Eden* (A Herbal Book). Loma Linda, CA, Back to Eden Books, 1946

Kraybill, Donald B., *The Riddle of Amish Culture.* Baltimore, MD, John Hopkins University Press, 1989

Lewis, Beverly, *October Song,* Minneapolis, Minnesota, Bethany House, 1949

Lewis, Beverly, *The Shunning*, Minneapolis, Minnesota, Bethany House XXXXXXXX

Lindsell, Harold, ed., *Harper Study Bible*, Revised Standard Version, Edited by NY, Harper and Row, 1962

Meyer, Joseph E., *The Herbalist.* Hammond, Indiana, Hammond Book Co., 1934

Miller, Levi, *Ben's Wayne,* Lancaster, PA, Good Books Co., 1989

Pellman, Rachel and Kenneth, *Amish Doll Quilts, Dolls and Other Playthings* Lancaster, PA, Good Books, 1986

Pellman, Rachel T. and Joanne Ranck, *Quilts Among The Plain People.* Lancaster, PA. Good Books, 1981

Ruth, John L., *A Quiet and Peaceable Life.* Lancaster, PA, Good Books 1979

Scott, Stephen, *The Amish Wedding.* Lancaster PA, Good Books, 1988

Scott, Stephen, *Why Do They Dress That Way?* Lancaster, PA. Good Books, 1986

Stroll, Joseph, David Luthy, and Elmo Stoll, editors, *Our Heritage* (8th grade reader). Aylmer, Ontario, Pathway Publishing Corp., 1980 (*c* 1968)

Van Braght, Thieleman J., *Martyr's Mirror.* Elkhart, Indiana, Mennonite Publishing Co., 1986

Zielinski, John M., *Amish Horse Farming Across America.* Iowa Heritage Publications, 1988

Internet Research

"Y2K disputes can use alternative dispute resolution—Firms need caution when hiring Y2K consultants," Headlines/Breaking News, www.bizjournals.com/site

Wangen, Jade, "Local woman serves others through alternative medicine," February 16, 2007, www.fillmorecountyjournal.com

www.kstp.com – Search – article/pstories/s11192.html 1/20/2006

http://news.bbc.co.uk – Search – Country profile: Oman,

www.barnresort.com

www.dnr.state.mn – Search –parks/Forestville

www.swarthmore.edu – Search – library/peace/conscientiousobjection/co%20website/ pages 10/26/2005

http://en.wikipedia.org – Search – Hussein of Jordan/wife Queen Noor

Government Documents

Minimum Standards for the Amish Parochial or Private Elementary Schools of the State of Ohio as a form of Regulations. Compiled and approved by Bishops, Committeemen and others in conference, 1992.

Minnesota Dept. of Education, 1991 *Education Laws,* Volume1, Chapters 117-125. Extract from 1991 MN Statutes, printed January 1992.

Minnesota Dept. of Health, "The Law, Rule and Other Related Materials Pertaining to Health, Morticians, Funeral Directors, Fees and Licensing" (Pamphlet). May 1992

Minnesota Statutes Annotated. Chapter 301, Private Cemeteries, pages 796-797.

U.S. Constitution, 1st Amendment, Bill of Rights

Interviews and Personal Letters

The Amish Community, of the Townships of Amherst, Canton, Harmony, Preston, and Cresco, Iowa, personal interviews, and shared written material, 2005 – 2007

Berkland, Donald (Superintendent at Fillmore Central Schools) seeking information of State Laws- 2006, telephone call, August 16, 2006

Deters, Warren (Retired Farm Equipment Dealer, Collector of 'Steel Wheel Era' farm machinery, 'Rusty Tractors and Unique Junk'), Personal and telephone interviews

Menikheim, Douglas K. (Adjunct Professor, St. Thomas University) Letters and telephone interview, 1992

Minnesota School Board Association, Telephone call, Aug. 16, 2006

State of Minnesota School Board, Telephone call, Aug. 16, 2006

Minnesota Dept. of Education, Telephone call, Aug.16, 2006

Acknowledgements

Without the cooperation of the Amish community, I could not have compiled the material for this book. Because of their trust in me, I was able to visit them in their homes and to receive their approval of my written text. It was a pleasure to once again work with such caring people.

There are also a number of English people to whom I feel indebted.

My first thanks must always go to my husband Loren, who has been very patient when I have been attached to my computer so much of the time. He has gone over much of the material with me and given me emotional support, encouragement, information, and constructive criticism when needed.

Thank you to my friend, Eileen Gierke, who did the illustrations for this book. I also want to give a special thank you to her son Scott Cain, who enhanced the pictures for her and indirectly for me at no cost. He was an angel in the background.

I am indebted to my friend, Carol Rhodes, who gave of her time unselfishly to the editing of the book. She and her husband Jon just returned from teaching in Japan where they had been for several years. Knowing she is now retired and back in their home in Harmony, I asked for her help. Her understanding of the written material was crucial. The commitment and the nurturing she gave to this project are much appreciated.

Gretchen Bollweg, who helped me with my first book *The Amish of Harmony*, applied her talents to this book as well. She did my layouts and put the printed material into book form. My thanks to Gretchen for her talent and her professional help.

I want to thank once again my friends Vernon and Paula Michel—to Vernon for giving me his time to extract information concerning many aspects of tourism's beginnings; to Paula for the news articles and for reading the manuscript and commenting on it from a reader's point of view. Paula edited my first book, *The Amish of Harmony.*

I wish also to extend thanks to:

Mavis Johnson for reading the material as a reader and friend; Marilyn Trouten for news articles; Stephanie Silvers, Harmony's community librarian; Mr. Wallace Deters for details about 'The Auction' story.